To Barbara

TAKING CHARGE
of YOUR LIFE

Florence Littauer

Other Books by Florence Littauer

Personality Plus
Personality Puzzle with Marita Littauer
Put Power in Your Personality!
Getting Along with Almost Anybody with Marita Littauer
Talking So People Will Listen with Marita Littauer
Shades of Beauty with Marita Littauer
Why Do I Feel the Way I Do? with Fred Littauer
Daily Marriage Builders with Fred Littauer
After Every Wedding Comes a Marriage with Fred Littauer
Freeing Your Mind from Memories That Bind with Fred Littauer
How to Beat the Blahs
Blow Away the Black Clouds
It Takes So Little to Be above Average
How to Get Along with Difficult People
Out of the Cabbage Patch
I've Found My Keys, Now Where's My Car?
Silver Boxes
Dare to Dream
Raising Christians, Not Just Children
Your Personality Tree (also available as video album)
Hope for Hurting Women
Looking for God in All the Right Places
The Gift of Encouraging Words

CLASS Books

Christian Leaders, Authors, and Speakers Seminar
   (tape, album, and manual)
The Best of Florence Littauer

TAKING
CHARGE
of YOUR
LIFE

Florence Littauer

Fleming H. Revell
A Division of Baker Book House Co
Grand Rapids, Michigan 49516

Published by Fleming H. Revell
a division of Baker Book House Company
P.O. Box 6287, Grand Rapids, MI 49516-6287

Previously published by Word Publishing as *Wake Up, Women!*

Printed in the United States of America

Library of Congress Cataloging-in-Publication Data

Littauer, Florence, 1928–
     [Wake up, women]
     Taking charge of your life / Florence Littauer.
          p.   cm.
     Originally published: Wake up, women. Dallas: Word Pub., c1994.
     ISBN 0-8007-5682-7 (pbk.)
     1. Assertiveness in women. 2. Sex role—Religious aspects—Christianity. 3. Women—United States—Social conditions. 4. Women—United States—Life skills guides. I. Title.
HQ1206.L56   1999
305.42′0973—dc21   98-143718

Unless otherwise indicated Scripture quotations are from the King James Version of the Bible.

Scripture marked NKJV is from the New King James Version. Copyright © 1979, 1980, 1982 by Thomas Nelson, Inc. Used by permission. All rights reserved.

Scripture marked NIV is from the HOLY BIBLE, NEW INTERNATIONAL VERSION®. NIV®. Copyright © 1973, 1978, 1984 by International Bible Society. Used by permission of Zondervan Publishing House. All rights reserved.

Scripture marked TEV is from *The Good News Bible,* the Bible in Today's English Version. Copyright © 1966, 1971, 1976, 1992 by American Bible Society. Used by permission.

Stories in this book are based on fact, and permission has been granted where appropriate for the stories' use. However, names and details have been changed to protect identities.

For current information about all releases from Baker Book House, visit our web site:
http://www.bakerbooks.com

Contents

Introduction

Am I a Christian "Dear Abby"?

I must have the kind of face people want to confess to. Or maybe I have a sign on my back announcing, "Free counseling here." Or perhaps I bear a striking resemblance to Lucy in the *Peanuts* strip, giving out "Help" for a nickel.

Everywhere I go people I don't even know pour out their hearts to me. Is there something about me, or are there really so many hurting people who don't think anyone cares? So many confused individuals looking for someone to question, someone who appears willing to listen? Would these same people confess to you if you gave them a chance? That's all I do. Perhaps you are like me. You smile and ask people how they are doing today, and they tell you.

One day this week I went Christmas shopping. I went first to the photographer to pick up some pictures I had ordered. When I entered he was sitting at his desk, his head in his hands.

"Is there something wrong?" I asked.

He looked up sadly and replied, "It's Christmas. That makes me think of my father. He died on Christmas Eve."

"Last year?" I asked.

"No, seven years ago."

It surprised me a bit that this man's grief would still be so consuming after that length of time, but I know from experience that any memory that hurts you is real and the last thing you need is for someone to say, "Snap out of it." So I listened as he told me about his father's last hours on Christmas Eve seven years ago. When he finished, he said he felt better and thanked me for caring.

Next I went to a gift shop that has exquisite pottery and china. When I asked the clerk who approached me to show me a crystal paper weight that was locked in a display case, neither she nor any of the other six clerks knew where to find the key. When I asked about a vase in the window, she informed me that she wasn't allowed to reach in there. It seems no one else was either. I never saw the vase. Despite the clerk's lack of ability to help me, I did buy several large pieces, and my clerk helped me carry them to the car. On the way there I asked who was in charge of the store.

"The manager," she told me.

"Which one was the manager?" I asked.

"Oh, you didn't see her. She sits in the back room. She doesn't like to deal with people."

I expressed that this manager's attitude was obvious and that I hoped they could straighten out their problems. Before I could get into the car, she took hold of my arm and asked, "What shall I tell the supervisor when she comes tomorrow? She's going to interview each one of us separately and I'm afraid to tell her the truth about the manager because I don't want to be fired."

"Why don't you quote me?" I suggested. "Put the blame on me by saying that a good customer asked who's in charge."

I went on to help her build a case by quoting customers' observations, a plan that would free her from personal criticism. She was delighted with the scenario and thanked me repeatedly as I got into the car. As I drove away she stood on the curb and waved good-bye.

A while later I went to Office Depot to pick up my Christmas cards. I had already become acquainted with the young woman in charge when I had placed my order the previous day.

She now came over to me immediately and announced, "I'm *so* glad to see you. You won't believe what's happened."

She went on to tell me that when she'd arrived home the previous night there was a note on the kitchen table from her husband saying that he didn't want to be married anymore. "He took all the money out of the bank account—money I'd saved up for Christmas for the kids—and he left town. 'Don't try to find me and have a Merry Christmas,' he wrote." She burst into tears, and I reached across the counter to comfort her as she vowed, "I'll never trust another man as long as I live."

As I drove home I thought about my day. I'd listened to a man still grieving over the death of his father, I'd given focus to a clerk afraid of losing her job if she told the truth, and I'd comforted an abandoned wife who had no money for Christmas. Did this happen because I was out looking for trouble or because there are hurting people everywhere who are looking for someone who cares?

One of my friends once told me that I'm a Christian "Dear Abby," and I guess maybe I am.

This book is intended to help women face the facts of where they are and use their intelligence and common sense to help them take charge of their lives. It will challenge women to face reality, function wisely, and bring their lives into balance.

The chapters ahead do not cover every problem a woman faces. Instead, they focus only on those areas where I find that women don't feel they have a right to question, areas where they have been taught ignorance is bliss. We can no longer assume we deserve to live happily ever after. We have to wake up, take responsibility for our lives, and move on to the best God has for us.

One woman, after hearing me speak, commented, "Your words gave me permission to confront a long-festering wound in my marriage. I had been ignoring it in hopes that it would go away, but it didn't improve until I used common sense and said, 'No more.' My children rallied around me and said, 'It's about time.' Together we faced the problem of spousal abuse and have taken steps to create a positive home atmosphere. Thanks for encouraging me to take control of my life and the emotional health of my children."

As a conservative Christian woman, a public speaker, an author, and a wife who has been married to the same man for more than forty years, I believe I can write from a view that is not radical but real, not women's liberation but women's liberty in the Lord. If you find yourself and your situation described in these pages, I pray that you will be helped by the experiences and lessons you find expressed here. Even if you aren't directly involved in a situation like those mentioned here, God will use this information to assist other women in your lives who are crying out for help to live a balanced Christian life. In the last chapter, I hope you will rediscover the source of strength that can help you turn your life around, no matter how troubled it is. Then your "Dear Florence" letter or that of someone you know can be a success story!

One **PART**

◆◆◆◆◆◆◆◆◆

PREPARING TO TAKE CHARGE

One

Back When Father Knew Best and We Left It to Beaver

Dear Florence:
  All around me people's lives seem to be falling apart. Are things really worse than they used to be or do I just remember the good old days with nostalgia?

Confused in Columbus

Dear Confused:

Yes, things are worse than they used to be. When you and I were young, there weren't as many opportunities to get into trouble as there are today. We accepted the basic laws of life as our parents presented them. We could see that when we behaved we got ahead, and when we didn't we got into trouble. Life was more structured and comfortably predictable.

We grew up with set rules that kept us in neat little boxes. We had two pairs of shoes, black for winter and white for summer, and we never wore the white ones before Memorial Day. We women wore hats to church, and we attended services each Sunday without question. Never did we think of saying, "I don't think I'll go to church today" or "I'd rather go to the beach." We wore our best dresses to church and never even thought of wearing slacks. No matter how poor any of us were, we all had our church clothes.

We ate routine meals and hadn't even heard the word *gourmet*. As I grew up in Massachusetts my family had set patterns for meals: Saturday night, without fail, was franks and beans accompanied by steamed, canned B & M brown bread. Apple pie with hefty chunks of Vermont cheddar cheese was always the dessert. No one ever seemed to be on a diet, and on Sunday morning we reheated the leftover beans and pie for breakfast. Before leaving for church we had to help stuff the little chicken so he'd be cooked by the time we got home. We had chicken every Sunday. Our heavy meal was at noon and was called dinner, and our lighter fare was our evening supper. Lunch was any snack at any time.

We were all expected to get married. There was no singles scene, so looking for a man was somewhat confined to college and church. Peculiar old-maid aunts were hidden away and brought out only to do the dishes after Christmas dinner.

Weddings were major social events and were especially important if the bride and groom came from two well-known families of merit in the community. All brides wore white and were considered beautiful, at least for the day. Couples started married life in little apartments—except for those who had wealthy parents—and borrowed furniture from anyone who would donate to their cause. We brides gave up our brief careers to dedicate our time and efforts to household management and raising children. Childless couples were viewed with compassion for their obvious deficiency.

As soon as possible, we rented a little tract house to give the children a yard. Eventually the big day would come when we could buy our first home. We fenced in the backyard and bought a puppy for the children. We purchased a little yellow plastic pool and a swing set, and when we could we added a playhouse or a fort. Right from the beginning we made plans to add on to the house, and we often discussed the future with friends who were also building creative wings in their minds. Sometimes we actually built an addition, which always included a family room with a fireplace and a large game table where we could work puzzles and play Monopoly. We never thought of going out to dinner. The early days of TV kept us at home for evenings with Milton Berle and Ed Sullivan.

Instead of being shuffled four times a week after school and on weekends to organized sports, competitive dance, and music lessons, our children happily played baseball in the empty lot next door or rode their bicycles until dark. Instead of long drives to out-of-town hockey games and meals on the road, weekends were spent in the yard with Dad and in church with the rest of the family and then to Grandma's house for dinner on Sundays. There was little sense of adventure, but we were warm, comfortable, and secure.

Marriage was a 'til-death-do-us-part commitment. If we weren't perfectly happy, we would never let anyone know it. "Never air your dirty laundry in public" was a firm family motto. Men earned the money, paid the bills, and decided who got what allowance. If a man looked at another woman, people commented on his roving eye. If he had an affair, a cloud of shame engulfed the whole family. Wives were expected to be dutiful homemakers. Flashing a seductive smile at the butcher could brand one as a fallen woman. Nice people never thought of divorce, and all we knew about stepmothers was confined to the wicked one in *Snow White*.

What we laugh at today in reruns of *Leave It to Beaver* and *Father Knows Best* was the norm for the time. We left our doors unlocked and never imagined that someone would steal our car. Drugs were aspirin and cough drops; social drinking was sipping champagne in the fruit punch at weddings. We didn't talk about morals and values; we lived them.

We loved God, motherhood, and apple pie, and we trusted each other. We didn't worry about damaging our children's self-esteem if we told them no, and they grew up knowing their limits. They learned that money didn't grow on trees. We'd all come out of the Depression and lived through the war, and we appreciated each new possession we acquired. We liked living where we grew up. We all knew each other and would ultimately retire and enjoy our forever friends into eternity.

Looking back, it all sounds so simple now.

Everything's Changing

Dear Florence:

I read in the papers about values and ethics being a thing of the past. I see that life is different today. I know that morals have disappeared. Did this happen overnight or did it sneak up on us?

Questioning in Quebec

Dear Questioning:

People's sets of values don't change overnight, but we learn gradually that what we believed to be true doesn't really matter that much anymore. Bit by bit we accept a broadening of our standards until we don't really have them any longer. I got married in the fifties. We had all lived through the Depression by hard work and putting ourselves through school. We had won the war to end all wars by sacrifice and scrap metal drives. We were ready to settle into predictable futures and we expected our children to be grateful for all we'd done for them. After all, we were living off the fruits of our labors. But somewhere along the line, gratitude left and judgment moved in.

Young people whose parents worked hard to provide them with substantial homes and quality education rebelled at the emphasis on keeping up with the Joneses and wandered off to spartan settings, scattering daisy petals along the way. These flower children became the Me Generation. Forget the old standards, they said. If it feels good, do it.

By the seventies the drug culture had emerged but was not considered a real problem; marijuana was thought to enhance clear thinking. The seventies were labeled the Age of Anxiety as people got increasingly nervous about finding themselves. Too late they realized that free love hadn't set them free.

By the eighties the baby boomers had grown into the yuppies. They put on suits, got real jobs, drove BMWs, drank Perrier, and seemed to like the feel of money. According to *Time* magazine, in the late eighties and early nineties twenty-two thousand magazine and newspaper articles featured the word *yuppie*.[1] The eighties became the Age of Avarice and produced corporate raiders and junk-bond kings.

The Greed Generation was in recession by the birth of the nineties. Yuppie columnist Walter Shapiro put it this way: "The yuppie mystique was built around a sense of generational entitlement that had its roots in the prosperity of the 1950s and '60s. In these more perilous times, there is an undeniable tempering of wanton consumption, but affluent baby boomers cannot cast off the experiences of a lifetime merely by switching outfits at the Gap."[2]

As sociologists look at the nineties they see the end of financial gain and high living. They have called this the Get Real Generation: Do whatever it takes to protect yourself. Don't worry about others. Now, as we look into a new millennium we find our nation without set rules or morals, with leaders who believe they can get away with anything as long as they have charm and look good. Do we really expect this to succeed?

Christians in a Crazy World

Dear Florence:

As I look at all the problems around me—divorces, drugs, immorality—I can't help but wonder where the church fits into all these changes. Have we zipped along with the world? Have we compromised our standards to keep up with the happy hedonists? Or have we held Christian standards high? As the yuppies have searched for self-identity and asked, "Who am I?" have we had the right answers?

A Christian in a Crazy World

Dear Christian:

What an appropriate question! We seem to have developed in different directions during these last decades. The church appears to be somewhat like an odd, oversized Dr. Seuss ostrich with three heads facing in opposing directions. One head is buried firmly in the sand of the fifties, another is stretching toward the future unshackled by old-fashioned rules of virtue and fidelity, and the third has decided to get real, face the issues of the day, not compromise standards, and look to Scripture for answers.

The media often features Christians as the buried-in-the-fifties head—negative, sour-faced, ignorant people holding a Bible in one hand while setting fire to the local adult bookstore or shooting doctors who do abortions with the other. These people, when interviewed, look like the pair in the American Gothic picture. Holding up a pitchfork, they spout damnation scriptures while appearing to be underpaid actors in *The Grapes of Wrath*. At best they come across as hapless victims of a cult leader who has obviously wiped out their minds and brainwashed their children.

Unfortunately, these characters often catch the media's attention, purporting to represent all Christians. One afternoon I flipped on the TV only to see a noted talk-show personality interviewing a group of nudists. They were sitting relaxed and confident while stark naked before the audience. For us home viewers they had placed little blurry spots over each person's strategic areas, but the dots didn't take the place of clothes. At the point I tuned in and stood shocked at the subject of the day, the host said, "And now for the Christian point of view on nudity in public." I held my breath as the camera panned to an overweight man in a T-shirt and plaid shorts. He was carrying a Bible and wearing a Donald Duck hat. As he began his astonishing monologue I decided he had to be an actor; no one could have been that bad spontaneously.

Was there any basis of truth in this caricature? Was the audience hissing at Christianity as well as this pathetic person? Are we still out of step with reality?

I can't help but feel that we Christians aren't quite ready to face the new millennium. Recently I talked with a pastor who explained why he was canceling the popular singles Sunday school class at his church. "It was growing so fast, and I could see it was bringing in people with problems. What we want here is sweet little families who will give to the church," he told me. Wouldn't we all like to leave it to Beaver!

The church's second ostrich head, which the press also loves to feature, is the one that has thrown all standards to the wind in an apparent orgy of sexual sin and financial finagling. How the media love to prove that pious believers are just like everyone else—only more phony! As one respected leader after another falls off his or her pedestal, the cause of Christ is increasingly diminished. And as the church labels unrepentant adulterers as good people who had a momentary indiscretion, we give our young people elastic options they shouldn't be offered.

But what about that third head of our ostrich, the balanced attitude that is moral yet not legalistic, real without abandoning rules, positive but not preachy, compassionate without running mascara? And where do women fit into this picture? Is it possible to be a positive, real, and intelligent woman and still stay in the church? Or should we remain the drab, dull little damsels who become doormats for the church foyers? Should we have no greater desire than to wash and dry communion cups in the church basement? Or should we throw in the towel and head out into the world to find ourselves? Can an intelligent Christian woman take control of her life without appearing worldly? Where is the balance?

This book offers some answers.

two

Filling Our Emotional Vacuum

Dear Florence:

My boyfriend and I are engaged. We are opposites in Personalities and don't agree on many issues. I want to talk about it, but he clams up and just says forget about it. Then I am sorry I ever brought it up. Will premarital counseling help us?

Wondering in Wisconsin

Dear Wondering:

Premarital counseling is helpful if each individual is open to learning personally and not just hoping the other partner will get the message. Counseling is only as good as the receptivity of the seekers.

When Fred and I got married in 1953, there was no such thing as premarital counseling. But we wouldn't have gone anyway. We thought we knew the right answers to everything. We looked good, we were equally educated, and we were faithful church attenders. It would have taken a pastor of great depth and insight to have spotted our problems ahead of time, for they were hidden in our emotional needs. We each came into marriage with empty suitcases that we expected the other to fill. The problem was we didn't know ourselves what we were after. Now, after years of study and teaching, we can share what we have learned.

We now know there are two major sources of emotional needs. The first is based on inborn desires that stem from our natural personalities, and the other is rooted in our individual family backgrounds.

I suggest you first read *Personality Plus* to understand your differences and then find a pastor or counselor who will help you communicate your needs to each other. If your fiancé clams up before marriage, he won't suddenly improve after the wedding.

Understanding the Personality Types

Dear Florence:

I've heard you talk about emotional needs. How can I put my finger on the needs of my personality and see if I am meeting those of my husband? Where do these needs come from anyway?

Needy in Needles

Dear Needy:

In the last ten years the field of genetics has grown in leaps and bounds. Experts can identify what we do and don't inherit and what comes from our environment. This "nature vs. nurture" study tells us we inherit our personality. I have written numerous books on the four basic personalities, so I will just review them here to refresh your memory.

The *Popular Sanguine* is the fun-loving, outgoing, optimistic, talkative personality. By nature these people have emotional needs that make them seem like perpetual children, and if these needs are not met in their family when they're young, they may never grow up emotionally. They may have adult bodies and minds, but emotionally they remain three years old. People say behind their backs, "Why, she's just like a child. Will she ever get her act together and grow up?"

No matter what age a Sanguine is, his or her needs are still inside, waiting to be met. The fewer needs that were met as a child, the more grabby he or she will be as an adult. Sanguines are desperate for *attention,* yet they usually marry Melancholies, who soon grow sick of listening to them. They want *approval* for every bit of trivia they manage to achieve, but their mates won't give them any compliments unless they become perfect. They want touchy-feely *affection* in front of their friends, but their Melancholy mates are repulsed by public displays of showy love. Sanguines have never felt *acceptance* from their families, so they believe their mates should accept them as they are right now, not as they might become years later if they happen to improve. When we look objectively at Sanguines' childlike emotional needs, we can see why they will do anything to please others. They are the most emotionally needy of all and frequently wonder, "Won't somebody love me as I am?" Their empty suitcase longs to be filled with approval, attention, affection, and acceptance.

The *Perfect Melancholy* is born desiring perfection and even as a child he or she gets depressed when things aren't right. Melancholies born into dysfunctional families are almost assured of emotional problems as they grow up. They constantly try to fix things but see no results. Because it's a natural tendency for them to want things done properly, they are often disappointed in people who don't seem to care. Melancholies tend to be highly organized, detail conscious, and analytical. They are usually the most artistic, musical, poetic, or philosophical in any group and tend to see things from an intellectual level. They can't find anyone perfect enough to marry, but they usually settle on the bubbling Popular Sanguine who they hope will cheer them up. Melancholies are desperate for *sensitivity* to their inner feelings yet they marry Sanguines, who don't see too far below the surface. For example, Fred used to say to me, "If you really loved me, you would know what I am thinking." But I had no idea what he was thinking, and I'd come out with some funny comment that would show him I was hopelessly out of touch. Melancholies also want *support* when they're down, which tends to be frequently, but their Sanguine mates, who can't stand gloomy people, tend to flee instead of lifting their sagging spirits.

Even Melancholy children like their possessions in order and don't like people to touch their things. Just imagine how depressing it is for a Melancholy to be married to a Sanguine who can't even find a pen that works or pair of scissors and who therefore rummages through the Melancholy's perfectly arranged drawers.

Melancholies also like *silence.* They are annoyed by loud chatty people, yet they often marry them. Just so much noise and they have to leave the room to find a place of silence. Surely a Melancholy must have written the slogan, "Silence is golden." For Sanguines, silence is dead air to be avoided at all costs. So when they see the prospect of a quiet night at home with their Melancholy mate, they quickly invite friends. The Melancholy can't stand all these people and longs for space of his or her own. The Melancholy suitcase wants to be filled with cozy silent spaces with a few occasional friends who are sensitive and supportive.

The *Powerful Cholerics* are the great achievers in the world. They love to work and need to be in control to feel secure. Where Sanguines love to talk and Melancholies like to analyze, Cholerics love to be in charge of whatever is available, whether or not they were asked to do so. The Choleric doesn't need to read the bylaws to become president.

Even though Cholerics don't appear to be emotional, they crave *appreciation* for all the work they have accomplished. If you don't notice what they've done, they'll point it out to you: "While the rest of you were wasting time, I finished building a wing onto the house." If you know what's good for you, you will rise up quickly and stand in awe: "I can't believe you accomplished so much in such a short time." With this comment the Choleric recognizes you as a person of discernment. Cholerics also demand loyalty among the troops, whomever the troops may be. Any sniff of mutiny will bring their wrath to the surface, so it's important that you throw in occasional sentences such as, "We're with you" or "We're on your side," even when you don't know what

the side is.

The Choleric who sees life in black and white—you're either with me or against me—usually marries a Peaceful Phlegmatic who lives in a haze of gray indecision. "It doesn't matter. I don't care. Whatever you like. You choose. Whatever's easy." The Phlegmatic is usually the only personality who can live with the Choleric and stay sane because he or she really doesn't care most of the time. "Look," the Choleric says, "notice how much I've done while you've been resting." The Choleric wants a suitcase filled with blue ribbons—awards for achievement from loyal and adoring fans.

Peaceful Phlegmatics are the easygoing, laid-back, agreeable people who get along with everybody and have no enemies. They know how to agree with whatever the Choleric proposes and appear to go along with them. They will smile and nod and say, "I'll be glad to do it" while underneath they're mumbling, "That'll be the day." Their pleasant facade often masks a quiet will of iron. The question they most loathe is, "When are you going to get up and do something?" They just wish you'd love them whether or not they stand up.

Phlegmatics bounce well with joy or adversity and all they want is a little *peace and quiet.* They have learned to smile when unhappy, listen without hearing, and sleep with their eyes open. They will put their greatest effort into saving effort. They would like to be accepted as decent people whether or not they do anything spectacular and they hope in the long run to be considered of *worth and value.* Quietly the Phlegmatic says, "Notice me." The Phlegmatic wants a suitcase that is sound-proofed and filled with pillows while a tape repeats, "You are worthy."

Can you see from this peek at the Personalities how close to hopeless it is for us to try to live together in harmony without an understanding of why we are so different from each other? As we have gone over the Personalities and their inherent emotional needs, I hope you have spotted yourself and those other people who are nothing like you. Ask yourself what your emotional needs were as a child. What was missing in your home that you cried out for? What lack or dysfunction affected your personality? What were you looking for as a teenager? Did this desire get you in any trouble? Did you choose a mate who was equally needy? Did you meet each other's needs in a positive way or a sick way? Did this marriage last? If not, did you repeat your mistakes? Are you handling your friends and coworkers with understanding?

If you need additional help in analyzing your personality type, read *Personality Plus, Personality Puzzle, Your Personality Tree,* or *Getting Along with Almost Anybody.* As you assess your personality, keep in mind that you may have elements of more than one type. For example, because of my Sanguine nature I needed Fred to pay attention to my every word, approve of everything I did, rave about me in public, and accept me as I was without constantly correcting me. And because of my Choleric nature I also wanted him to appreciate how hard I worked and to keep his eyes loyally on me alone. Since we didn't understand any of this and I couldn't articulate these needs, Fred didn't begin to meet them. His Melancholy nature made him believe that if he worked hard enough on me I would become perfect and have no peculiar needs that he would have to meet. He also had Choleric needs for credit and loyalty. He felt I was insensitive and unsupportive and I, of course, had no desire for the silence he craved. When we look back on those first fifteen years of marriage, we are amazed that we hung in there. We also see why so many couples with no tools of understanding give up on each other and come to believe they could be happy if they had a different mate. Because of the changes that came to us when we began to study the Personalities, we have dedicated the past thirty years to helping other couples see the light.

Is your suitcase still empty? Are you so anxious for fulfillment that you might start looking for love in all the wrong places? Do you know what your mate is looking for? It is usually quite opposite from your needs. If you don't understand each other, talk it over today. What is each personality pattern? What similarities or differences do you have? What unmet needs do you have that the other has not filled? Don't use this time of discussion for an attack, but as time to improve loving relationships. Talk about this with close friends and your children as well. Often friendships and sibling relationships improve when we see that just because someone is different doesn't make him or her wrong.

Differences in Family Backgrounds

Dear Florence:
You said that family backgrounds are also a source of emotional needs. How important is that factor?
Franny in Frankfort

Dear Franny:

Each of us is born with a personality that needs nourishment to mature. The second source of concern comes from our individual family background. Adding these two together can create people who are looking desperately for emotional fulfillment without being able to articulate what they're after. The broader our differences in personality and family background, the less apt we are to understand each other's needs. This is especially true when it comes to needs generated by different family backgrounds. Such needs can lead to unfulfilled expectations in marriage.

Fred grew up in the lap of luxury from my point of view. He had all the things I didn't have: the huge English Tudor home, separate bedrooms for each child, imported German domestic help, expensive cars, and plenty of money. When I first saw where he lived, I said to myself, *Florence, this is for you!*

What I didn't see was Fred's need for someone to love him and make him feel significant. He was the middle of five children and somehow he seemed to continually fall through the cracks. Added to those feelings of rejection was baggage from being sexually abused.

When we add up all of Fred's needs, we now realize I married an emotional time bomb who wanted someone to love him and support him. Under his charm and sophistication was a boiling anger. He kept it under control almost all the time but I knew it was there, and I also knew how to tiptoe around it to prevent eruptions.

I came into this marriage wide-eyed and innocent, just wanting to have a good time. I had been forced to grow up early in life as I **27** had been responsible for meeting many of my two brothers' needs and for mothering my mother when my father died. Since we lived in a store with people around us from 6:30 A.M. until 11:00 at night, I got plenty of attention; people praised me for everything I did and I was considered the most intelligent girl around. My report cards were posted in the store and my father had always bragged about how well I did each term. My natural Sanguine and Choleric needs were met, but we had none of the things I wanted and read about in romance novels. We had no car, no phone, no bathtub, no hot water, and no money. I frequently wished, *If only I could have a normal house with a front door, a lot of clothes, and plenty of money . . .*

So many of us marry someone who appears to fill our emotional vacuum. Here I was, hungry for houses and money and willing to love someone who'd give it to me, and Fred had the money and was desperate for love. As we look back on it, we see our attraction to each other was partly because of our perception that the other person had what we needed.

So many of us, having no knowledge of the differences in personalities and the collection of emotional needs we carry around with us, have no healthy way to analyze ourselves.

How about you? What emotional needs came out of your childhood? What were you deprived of that you still long for inside? When Fred and I first discussed our needs, he didn't think that my desire for a house, clothes, and money could be considered an emotional need. That's because he grew up with plenty of clothes and money while I felt deprived in that area, having to wear charity clothes and with only enough money for meals. We began to realize that my needs were his strengths, while his needs were my strengths. No wonder we didn't understand each other!

Fred and I are so grateful that after fifteen years of a deteriorating marriage we began to study the Personalities. This concept gave us the tools we needed to rebuild our lives. Later we came to understand our different emotional needs, and we began to repair the hurts we'd put upon each other. I could see that when Fred gave me plenty of money and clothes and we lived in a big house I was willing to give him a portion of the love he needed, but when he had financial problems, I withdrew my love and support at a time when he needed them the most. We didn't mean to be self-centered and emotionally greedy, but we had no wisdom to call upon, no course to take, no books to read.

We are so grateful today that the Lord has blessed us in spite of ourselves and has used our mistakes, our misunderstood needs, and even Fred's childhood molestation to give us a sensitivity to others' needs and a desire to be used to help others.

Emerging from Never-Never Land

Dear Florence:

Am I right that most couples get married without objective counseling? My sister says that if you are in love everything else will work out. But I see friends who seem happy before they are married and then get into problems soon after. Don't they ask each other the right questions? Why does every bad situation seem to be a surprise? I have not been married yet, and I'm not sure I'd take the chance.

Single in Seattle

Dear Single:

I don't blame you for being afraid to tackle marriage. You are right; many couples don't ask touchy questions ahead of time. They hope, as your sister says, that being in love will be enough.

Our work in helping troubled husbands and wives would be much simpler if couples came to us *before* the wedding. Then we could help them understand the Personalities and the potential impact of past events on their lives. With that understanding they could anticipate and resolve problems those issues might create in their marriage. But far more often we get cries for help after the honeymoon (and after several months or years of marriage). That was the case with Lynn, who poured out her life to me after a seminar.

Lynn came out of an abusive childhood and an abusive marriage. She was glad to escape from a vicious beating, to run off with her two children, and finally be free. She had no choice but to work **29** hard to support them because her ex-husband had left the state and she had no way to find him. She had been a victim all her life and she accepted her plight as what she deserved. Her husband had been an atheist and wouldn't let her go to church, so somewhat in a late rebellion she decided to join a local church. She was so angry over her circumstances that she refused to participate in any activities until she read in the bulletin about a support group for the "Depressed and Done In." Immediately she mused, "If anyone's been depressed and done in, it's me."

The support group was more depressive than she had anticipated, and Lynn wouldn't have returned a second week if it hadn't been for that one single man who sat quietly, appearing to analyze the rest of the participants. He had smiled at her once and somehow that one smile was enough to make her go back the next week. She spent a little extra time on her hair and makeup and tried to appear happier than she really was. Lynn managed to sit next to Ben this time and she tried to engage him in conversation. He was so quiet and shy and such a contrast to her ex-husband, who yelled at her every time she didn't please him.

In the following weeks as the group members opened up and shared their individual traumas, Lynn learned that Ben's wife had left him for a younger man and yet had managed to strip him of all his possessions. Lynn's heart went out to him. Here was someone who needed her; here was a gentle, soft-spoken Christian. Lynn thought to herself, *Finally, a male who's not out to control me.* Ben was not only not controlling, he didn't want to make any decisions at all. "Whatever you want to do" or "Whenever you want to go" seemed to be his mottoes. Lynn liked this Phlegmatic attitude and was so thrilled to have found a man with a passive personality. Cheerfully she activated a relationship with this man who needed her. She was able to sublimate her hate and bitterness over her first husband as she put her energy into salvaging this downtrodden soul.

Women coming out of abusive marriages and seeking gentle men could learn from Lynn's experience. As objective observers we can see several potential problems in this relationship. First, Lynn was looking to a new marriage to solve her problems and make her happy, but she had not yet begun to get over the emotional toll the past marriage had taken from her. She had not dealt with her own anger or the results of the abuse she had suffered for years. She had not even asked the question, "Why did I stay in that marriage so long?" nor had she discovered her sick need to be victim and savior to others in similar situations.

Lynn had gone back to church for the wrong reason; she wanted to show her ex she could go to church if she wanted to, even though he was not around to observe her rebellion. Lynn had not even tried to apply the Scriptures to her life problems. In fact, frequently she got angry at the pastor when he inferred all Christians could be joyful.

"If he'd lived my life he wouldn't be so happy," she would mutter.

Lynn felt she couldn't pray to a God who had allowed her to be beaten, and she knew that reading a few verses a day wasn't going to make that much difference either. The best thing about church, she thought, was finding a new mate who would make her happy. She could put the past behind her and start anew.

The second foreseeable problem Lynn faced as she began her new relationship was that she lacked knowledge about the basic Personalities. She didn't understand that she was Sanguine, the fun-loving type, and also Choleric, the one who wants to be in control. Lynn was depressed not only because of her circumstances but also because her life had never been fun and had been constantly out of her control. She didn't realize that she had perked up because she saw some ray of fun in the future with a new, kind man and had found someone who seemed willing to let her be in control.

If she had been aware that Ben was Phlegmatic, low-key and inoffensive, and also a little Melancholy, desiring perfection and getting depressed when not finding it, she could have foreseen the potential problems. She could have thought through the possibility that while she liked his gentle spirit she might have trouble living with his weaknesses. He might be lacking in ambition and frequently feel defeated and depressed. When we have a knowledge of the Personalities, we can anticipate a potential mate's **31** strengths and weaknesses and evaluate our ability to handle them. Was Lynn prepared to handle Ben's collective weaknesses on top of her own untended bitterness and anger? Would it all somehow work out in the long run?

The third problem was Lynn's lifetime of victimization. A multitude of studies in the '90s showed us that once abused, a person often falls into a downhill spiral of repeated victimization. Scripture tells us that the sins of the fathers are visited upon the children up to the third and fourth generation. The stench of abuse that has not been dug up, looked at, prayed over, and thrown out will rise to overwhelm future relationships. Lynn had put her energies into suppressing her hurts and trying to pretend they'd never happened.

Although victimization takes a toll on everyone, the personalities handle it differently; Phlegmatics and Melancholies like Ben tend to withdraw, say little, become introspective, achieve below their ability, and manifest depressive symptoms. Sanguines and Cholerics try to deny it ever happened, charge forth to overachieve, show themselves that these past problems can't hold them down, and become the saviors of other lost souls. This latter problem has been labeled as *codependency,* the process of being responsible for the destructive behavior of another person.

Lynn had no understanding of victimization and did not realize that her desire to pull Ben out of his miseries was feeding her own sick needs of rescuing someone in worse shape than herself. Lynn also didn't realize the principle that Fred and I have repeatedly seen proven over the years, that people tend to marry mates of opposite personality but who are on the same level of emotional health. Lynn, by nature an optimistic Sanguine with Choleric drive, was attracted to the gentle Phlegmatic Ben with his Melancholy reserve. Unfortunately, in marriage we wed the opposite strengths and don't realize we have to live with opposite weaknesses. When we understand this ahead of time, marriage is not such a rude shock; but when we don't, we fall into unexpected disappointments.

On the emotional level, we are attracted to people who have a similar amount of personal pain. Even though one mate may appear to be more stable than the other, underneath there is usually a well of bubbling symptoms seeking out a balancing pool of pain. We have found that an emotionally stable, mature, responsible individual will not be attracted to a potential mate who is emotionally unbalanced.

Looking at all of these potential problems with knowledge, any one of us could have predicted what was going to happen to Lynn and Ben. Pour all their problems into a large mixing bowl and add to it a portion of misdirected Christian platitudes on submission, money matters, and husbandly headship and you will produce a partnership of despair.

Lynn proposed marriage to Ben. She told us she had to propose as Ben wouldn't have thought it up on his own. The truth is somewhat different. She thought marriage would heal her hurts and make her happy. He didn't want to get married because he was still in pain from the rejection he'd experienced. He was in deep financial trouble and couldn't bear any additional responsibility. Lynn wouldn't hear of his objections though, and in a foolhardy spirit of love conquers all, she dragged him to the preacher, who gave them a booklet on the perfect Christian marriage: The husband works to support the family, handles all the money, and makes the decisions. The wife is submissive to his every whim, never questions his handling of the money, and stays home to prepare him nutritious meals. These ideas might work for a sweet spiritual couple who get married for the first time, understanding each other's strengths and weaknesses and carrying no emotional or financial baggage from the past. But does that represent Lynn and Ben?

Lynn was so eager to get married that she didn't discuss many of the basics of life with Ben. Naturally he didn't initiate any questioning of his disastrous finances and hadn't mentioned the child-support payments he was obligated to keep current. Lynn had an hourly job that barely fed her. She hated the work she was doing even though she had been promoted to supervisor, so once she married Ben she quit her job. She took the little booklet to heart and stayed home in the apartment to cook and clean.

Ben didn't tell her he was in debt and couldn't support her, so when she quit her job he panicked. But instead of confessing to her, he withdrew and got increasingly depressed. She tried to be the **33** happy housewife and cheer him up, but the more giddy she became the more miserable he was. As the unquestioning, submissive mate she was trying to be, Lynn didn't meddle in the finances. She just handed him the bills once a month. After all, aren't husbands supposed to support and protect their wives? Didn't the booklet talk about the husband as priest, provider, and protector?

It was at this point that Lynn came to one of our seminars where she learned about the Personalities for the first time. She saw her desperate need for fun and attention and realized she was getting neither. She saw that she had been out of control her whole life when her Choleric nature wanted so eagerly to be in charge.

That day we spoke on victimization as well as personality types, and I made the statement that those who were abused in childhood tend to develop a victim personality and continue to be victimized throughout life. This thought kept playing in Lynn's mind: Don't spend the rest of your life waiting for the other person to change. Take control of your life and ask the Lord to show you what he wants you to do.

A few weeks later Lynn's world fell apart one more time. She called to tell us the lights were turned off, the phones were disconnected, and the bank had called to report that several checks had bounced. All of Lynn's years of bottled up anger came spewing forth when Ben walked in the door that night. She attacked him in a rage, beat him over the head with a chair, knocked him to the floor, and jumped on him. She screamed, swore at him, and collapsed in a hysterical heap. Although Lynn uttered not a coherent word, Ben gathered that his fears had come to pass. Lynn knew about the money problems.

Ben locked himself in the bathroom and refused to come out to face his hostile, screaming wife. Here were two well-meaning people in what appeared to be a hopeless situation. When Lynn called for help she didn't know what to do and we were the only people she could think of who might understand. Fred was able to counsel them once they calmed down. He explained to them four basic problems that wouldn't necessarily be solved even if they had an

abundance of money.

1. *They got married too quickly and for the wrong reasons.* They didn't take time to get to know each other and especially didn't talk about money. They avoided touchy issues before marriage and then handled each one explosively as it reared its ugly head later. They had no basis for honest communication, and neither one wanted to discuss money.

2. *They had no understanding of their own personalities and even less of each other's.* They didn't know that under stress she would attack and he would pull back. They didn't realize that personality weaknesses burdened by the additional load of victimization become accentuated in a negative direction. Thus, what would have made a normal Choleric person angry infuriated Lynn into a wild display of temper and attack. What would have merely upset a normal Phlegmatic facing a confrontation threw Ben into a panic and caused him to run for cover. He had no defenses left.

3. *Neither one thought their childhood traumas had any bearing on their adult emotions.* They had each buried the past. Ben had refused to even think about his, and Lynn had pushed her past under a flurry of activity and codependent behavior. Even though Lynn had married a man who didn't beat her, she was being quietly victimized by his lack of financial responsibility and his hiding of the truth rather than facing it.

4. *Lynn wanted a Christian marriage so badly that she did everything the marriage booklet said without balancing it with common sense.* She quit her job without looking at their finances realistically. She put all the responsibility onto Ben with no knowledge of whether he wanted to handle it or was able to do so. She thought avoiding reality was part of submission and that her wishful thinking of having a strong, sound, reliable husband would make it all come true.

Does any of this sound familiar? There is no quick fix. So how could we help this distraught couple?

It was too late to repair problem number one. They were already married. Even so, we saw that they needed to be aware of and learn to understand each other's family background and personality. So **35** we explained their personality strengths and weaknesses, reviewed how opposite they were from each other, and reminded them, "Just because you're different doesn't make you wrong." These were new thoughts, especially to Ben, and understanding them helped both spouses see the reason behind their behaviors.

Getting to the core of their problems helped them to see why they put themselves into positions where they could be revictimized.

Perhaps the most painful part of their recovery was taking a realistic look at their finances. When they put the figures on paper, there was no hope but bankruptcy unless they were both willing to get to work and budget out a way to pay off the debts. They had both lied to each other over the money situation (Lynn also had some debts she had been reluctant to discuss). Neither one was totally right or totally wrong, but they both had to grow up, become responsible, and communicate daily about their problems until they were settled.

Two hurting people together don't automatically produce a happy marriage, as Lynn and Ben found out. But with God's help mismatched mates can overcome the odds that seem to be stacked against them. This begins with each spouse's taking responsibility for his or her recovery from the past instead of blaming the other. Lynn is taking control of her own life in a healthy way whether or not Ben changes. She recently told me, "I'll never forget that day at your seminar when you said, 'Wake up, women. Take charge of your lives.' I didn't know then how much I had to wake up to!"

three

Who Are All Those Dysfunctional People?

I once had a dysfunctional washing machine. It worked; it even washed and rinsed the clothes. The problem came in the spin cycle when water spurted out onto the floor making little streams across the linoleum. The top of the drum had rusted out, so when the spin hit high speed, the water became geysers. The machine functioned, but not as it was designed to do. The word *dysfunction* doesn't mean that we can't function at all. It means that we can't function as we are supposed to. Many of our families are managing, but not as they want to be. Some of us women are rusted out and get dizzy when we move into high speed. We function, but not as we expected, not as the Lord intended.

Dear Florence:

The other day one of my close friends said to me, "You have a dysfunctional family." We all have our quirks, but we get up each day and go to work. Even though I'm on my third husband who drinks a lot, I've kept my children stable and they've not done any worse than other teens. I was very hurt when my friend called us dysfunctional. What does that mean?

Woeful in Wabash　　**37**

Dear Woeful:

Your friend was unkind to be critical, but perhaps she was trying to alert you to some problems. We like to think that dysfunctional families live somewhere else. They drink a lot, have children on drugs, and never go to church. Books are written about them, but we don't think we need to read them. Some of them are labeled codependent, and many of them are involved in twelve-step programs and support groups. We are so glad we are not one of them!

But let's look again. Is there any chance that you are living in a situation that is somewhat off balance? Is there a chance that you are living in a state of denial, smiling as you refuse to look the truth in the face? Did your friend want to help you?

So many of us quote verses on honesty to our children. We know God wants us to be truthful in our innermost parts. We know the truth will set us free. We can recite the Ten Commandments and teach Sunday school, but some of us hope no one will peek underneath our blanket of deception and catch a corner of the real truth. Has your friend seen something that you have hidden even from yourself?

It's not that we ever intended to lie, but due to our circumstances we sometimes cover up the truth in order to cope. Some of us have come out of contentious homes that we told ourselves were normal. Some of us are in marriages where we are demeaned and verbally abused, and we're hoping the children won't notice, the church won't find out, and our friends won't see. Some who write to me are single mothers trying to raise their children, earn enough money to support them, and not be bitter about an ex-husband living happily in a comfortable lifestyle that's way above his means.

Whatever our situation, we need to wake up, face the truth, and take control of our lives so we can move on. We can't have faith in the future until we can acknowledge the present and look at ourselves with a realistic and appraising eye.

Are you in denial about some areas of your past and present?

Are you pretending that life is better than it is or that it will clear up tomorrow?

Are you looking the other way to avoid seeing what your friend has noticed?

Could you possibly be one of those dysfunctional people?

I would suggest that you ask yourself these questions. Then go to your friend and ask her what she meant. Listen; don't be defensive. Weigh what she says and correct whatever you can. Take a new control of your life.

The Barrier of Denial

Denial is refusing to accept the truth or disclaiming responsibility for unpopular or negative actions. It is the major barrier that prevents women from seeking counseling to uncover the root of their problems. Until the seeker is willing to face the truth, whatever it may be, there is little anyone can do to help her.

Tuning Out Abuse

Dear Florence:

I grew up in a home where no one but me seemed to be phased by my father's harsh outbursts. How can others be so unaffected? And what can I do now?

Alone in Abilene

Dear Alone:

Your question is shared by many who have grown up in similar homes. I remember one woman whose story you may find helpful.

Virginia grew up in an extremely religious home. Her mother was spiritually submissive, and Virginia and her sisters were trained to have "the attitude of a servant." Her father and brothers were considered superior to docile females and were never held to any accountability. Virginia never married and felt ill at ease in the presence of men.

When she came to one of our seminars, Virginia told me she had been abused by her older brother. She had never discussed the abuse with anyone, choosing instead to suppress the painful memories. After sharing her memories with us, Virginia listened to our teaching on the Personalities. Then she went home and explained **39** them to her Phlegmatic mother as a way to open up some genuine communication and put an end to her years of denial. Later Virginia wrote to me:

> Last week my mom and I had the first deep talk we've ever had. Three members of my family are rather low emotionally just now, and Mama asked about them. Talking about their situations really opened the door to explaining and discussing many things that had occurred in our family, including the many rejections, both verbal and more subtly. Mama remembers so few of these incidents that I realized anew how Phlegmatic she really is. I believe she tuned out and never really heard or absorbed the harsh statements and controlling threats Pop so frequently made to us.
>
> She doesn't remember things I recall happening when I was five or six. She doesn't realize how abused her children have been and therefore has never raised a finger in their defense.
>
> *She listened so well* as I explained about personalities. She could pick herself out as a Phlegmatic with some Melancholy in her. The outline of temperaments gave me an excellent background for two and a half hours of talking. I could sense the things I'd heard from you coming out of me—flowing out of me—and it was exhilarating! There were flashbacks where I could see you standing up there speaking and it was thrilling to realize that I, too, was able to speak in a confident, caring way. Thank you for helping me get beyond the denial. The truth does set us free.

Virginia's right. Don't waste any more time. Talk honestly with your family about your feelings. Then you too can be free.

Looking the Other Way

Dear Florence:

I was abused as a child and my mother pretended not to notice. When I tried to tell her, she said I was lying. I gave up and tried to deny what was happening myself. When I hit forty I had some severe depression and ignored my teenage daughter's complaints. Am I my mother all over again? Have others ever wondered the same thing?

Depressed in Denver

Dear Depressed:

Many write to me to say "My mother looked the other way and tuned out the abuse going on in the family. Now I'm afraid I've done the same thing." As mothers we must be aware of what's happening to our children and watch for signs of emotional or sexual abuse. We cannot look the other way when our children show signs of abuse; it's imperative to take action because the results of it don't go away. The symptoms grow worse and often seem to reach their peak around age forty, as you mentioned, suddenly causing the childhood victim to have sexual, emotional, and even physical problems that seem to appear without explanation. Many women tell us about years of counseling and medical tests that have not yet uncovered the source of their symptoms, which include failed marriages, migraine headaches, depression, PMS, and general dysfunction.

No one likes to think that his or her child could be abused. The tendency is to hope for the best, and optimism is always good; but we must be aware of the possibility of abuse, read up on the symptoms, and not leave the child with someone he or she pulls away from or reacts against.

When I ask mothers who suspected their children were being abused why they did nothing about it, they say, "It was easier to look the other way." Some add, "I didn't want to do anything that would upset my family" or "my husband" or "my mother." They say, "It was just better to pretend everything was all right and not to bring it up." Another excuse is "I didn't know how I could support the family without him," a realistic problem if the father ends up in jail. Another excuse is, "If I told him I suspected anything, he'd kill me." And those mothers who were victimized themselves as children say, "I lived through it so I guess she can too."

There is no easy way to deal with these problems when they invade our homes, but we must put the safety of the child before money, fear, indifference, or keeping the peace. We must come out of denial and seek the truth because while we are in denial, our **41** problems continue to grow. We need to watch for the symptoms and not put our religious heads in the sand.

Abuse isn't the only thing people ignore. A woman named Marie came up to my husband, Fred, at a lunch break during a workshop and told him about her daughter. Fred listened as Marie shared bizarre tales of a thirteen-year-old who was depressed and suicidal, who cut herself with razor blades and stuck pins through the ends of her fingers. She and her friends dressed totally in black and went to secret meetings. When she came home she seemed drugged and went immediately to her room, which was covered with posters of rock stars and witches. Her best friend at that point was in the hospital recovering from a suicide attempt. Would you say we had a serious problem here? No matter what your knowledge of satanic groups might be, could you not see that this child's behavior was way beyond any normal teen activity?

Fred explained the severity of the situation, telling Marie her daughter was probably involved in some occult or satanic activity. Her clothes, posters, behavior, and depression pointed to some form of mind control. Fred asked the mother what she'd done for the child and she said her doctor had given her mood-elevating drugs.

"Did they help?" Fred asked.

"I don't really know," Marie replied. "I found out she sold the pills at school."

"What did you do when you found that out?"

"There was nothing to do; she'd already sold them."

In frustration, Fred explained what she had to do to save this child. But when he challenged her to action, she responded, "My husband would never believe any of this. We're Christians and he doesn't take any stock in this satanic stuff." When Fred emphasized the seriousness of the suicide attempts, Marie shook her head. "My husband thinks it's just a phase and since I'm a submissive wife, I can't do anything about it," she said.

Is this what God means by submission? Ignoring a life and death situation to humor a husband in denial? Don't be like Marie!

Start by asking your daughter privately about any possibility of abuse, letting her know you love her and won't be upset. Tell her you had such problems yourself and you want to help her. If she admits abuse, get her to a Christian counselor who knows how to deal with these problems and won't just make her feel guilty. And take the necessary steps to stop any ongoing abuse.

Facing the Truth

I had just started writing this book when I first met Georgia. She was pouring all her energy into rearing her children and working as an artist. Emotionally she was just beginning to realize her life was coming apart at the seams. The denial system she had utilized for so many years was no longer working. Yet when asked how she was doing, Georgia would smile and say, "Just fine." As a Christian, Georgia put up with the pain of an abusive marriage because she felt she had no choice. After she finally faced the situation head-on, she wrote the following letter:

Dear Florence:

I was putting off my situation for too many years. I am so blessed that the Lord is restoring those years and healing the pain in my life and my children's, but many of the painful experiences could have been avoided if I had had the tools and the healing I have now.

Because of the life patterns I felt comfortable with, I could not see beyond the denial. That's why getting help is of the utmost importance. To be set free, truth *is the only avenue. Perhaps your book will open women's eyes to truth. Our Lord did not intend for us to be victims. Without truth we do not even know that we are* victims. *It has been a journey for me, and with each new truth there is new pain. But each time the pain is less, the* joy *more exhilarating. Hope and trust are new roads that I now travel with excitement and new expectation.*

Write your book. If it sets but one person on a journey to truth and the freedom that truth promises, then you will have been an instrument in the hands of our Lord. For He came that we might know the truth and be set free. And when one knows the truth then others follow. Because I've finally faced the truth, the lives of my children are being changed, and I know my grandchildren will someday experience a better way to live. Thank you for making me see the truth and take charge of my life.

Georgia in Atlanta

Pretending

The word *pretend* comes from the Latin roots that literally mean "to stretch in front of like a curtain." Pretending is a conscious act of believing things are better than they really are, that we really can live happily ever after. It's all right in fairy tales, but not in real life.

In an article titled "Psyched Out," author Mary Kay Blakely writes of the state of denial we seem to be in as a country. She tells of another article she wrote in which she suggested that people with problems face the true issues and not look for a quick fix. But the magazine editor wouldn't print the article because it wasn't optimistic enough, an attitude Blakely calls the Valium Theory of writing, giving people what they want to hear. This theory suggests that "prose should numb the blues without trying to name the problem."[1] She realizes the fallacy of teaching the public that happiness is within everyone's reach forever. Our first task in getting our lives together, she writes, is to get out of denial and "acknowledge reality."

If we picture life as a theatrical production where we all live happily ever after, we are pretending. We create a fictional fairy tale and step out from behind the curtain for our final bow. No one could have acted this out any better than I did. As a perfect candidate for Cinderella, I read all the fiction about the poor waif who married the handsome prince—and I did it. When Fred constantly corrected me and tried to make me perfect, I just smiled and moved on.

When We Could No Longer Pretend

Dear Florence:

My husband and I have struggled for three years to have a child. We've exhausted nearly every infertility treatment and lost four babies. We're nearly at the end of our rope. Sometimes it seems the easiest thing to do is to try to forget about it all and pretend things are back to the way they were before we knew we couldn't conceive. What should we do?

Hopeless in Hastings

Dear Hopeless:

I know what you mean when you say it seems easier to pretend there isn't a problem. When our first son was diagnosed as fatally brain damaged, both Fred and I made the best of it. In fact we did our best to deny it! Our families could handle it much better if we didn't talk about our producing this hopeless child, and few of them ever came near. It was easier to look the other way. We went to a healer who told us if we would only believe this child was perfect, he would be healed. I worked hard at pretending, but when the baby was screaming in convulsions, my faith in the healer fled.

We couldn't actually deny the reality, but we worked at pretending that tomorrow would be a brighter day. Optimism is a blessing, but while we are reaching for it we need to deal with the realities of today.

Our family had a double dose of reality when our second son was diagnosed with the same disease. I wanted to stretch a curtain over this second scene, but I had no choice. There was no happy ending. Both boys died. There was no curtain call, just an empty crib. We had to accept the fact that we had lost our two sons and make adjustments in our plan for our life together. Through this experience we both accepted the Lord and found *true reality.*

We talk with people every day who are not in touch with reality. Some are denying they have problems. And they'd rather not seek the truth. Some recognize the sad situation they are in but pretend it's not there so they won't have to deal with it. But neither denial nor pretending is an answer. Why? Because the pain, hurt, rejection, anger, guilt, and grief we are avoiding does not really go away. In fact, when ignored, these problems continue to worsen over time and always surface in other areas of our lives, creating even more trouble. To stop **45** the trouble, we must face the truth, work positively toward a solution, and learn from the experience.

Lives Built on Dreams

Dear Florence:

I am not a negative person and I believe that people are basically good. I do not want to go around being pessimistic and suspicious of others; it goes against my happy-go-lucky nature. I think it's good that I see the positive side of people, but I guess I have to admit that it gets me into trouble. It seems all the men I have ever dated or been involved with turn out to be liars, and even though I trusted and believed in them, they have used me and hurt me. I am starting to think that maybe I need to get real about people, but I am sad and even a little angry that life is not the way I dreamed it would be. What can I do about it?

Naive in Nashville

Dear Naive:

While it's good to have an optimistic nature, those of us blessed with that temperament need to be careful we don't slip into a dream world where we expect nothing bad will ever happen or that no one will ever hurt or betray us. If we insist on living in this "La La Land," we will most certainly be led on by lying Lotharios or duped by dashing Don Juans.

One morning I tuned into a talk show where the host was interviewing a young lady, I'll call her Leslie, who seemed to be attracted to charming men who would sponge off her and never go to work. Leslie wasn't a stupid woman academically. She had an MBA degree and a high-paying job. She had lived with one particular man for five years and had a child by him; she had given him money, checks, and credit cards. She looked the other way when he had affairs and broke up with him only when his lavish spending on other women caused her to go bankrupt. But Leslie didn't seem to learn from this disaster. She soon went into another relationship with a man of culture, refinement, and the arts who sat home and thought about what he might write or paint.

When asked what she had learned from all this she said, "To look at their bank accounts and employment records before I get involved." Leslie had built her life on a dream, living a life of pretense even when the truth was standing in front of her, waving a red flag. She refused to give up on her idea of how the world *should* be!

Leslie was just a passing face on TV, but I have met many women whose stories are similar to hers, women who built their lives on dreams and refused to see the truth. Like me, many women grew up optimistic, wanting the best and expecting to get married and live happily ever after. We were instructed to compliment people who weren't attractive, to smile when we felt like crying, and to deny that we had any problems at home. So is it any wonder now that we look the other way when our dream husband disappoints us and our children are far from perfect? Don't we also hope that if we hang in there one more day our circumstances will change?

Dr. Harriet Lerner, author of *Dance of Deception*, says, "Pretending is so closely associated with femininity that it is, quite simply, what the culture teaches women to do." In her book she issues a call for women to become honest with themselves if they wish to have any kind of positive, intimate relationship with anyone. "Lying erodes trust," Dr. Lerner points out. "Closeness requires honesty."[2] How can you have a genuine relationship with someone you can't trust?

Becoming Real

Dear Florence:

When I was growing up, I saw my mother as bossy and domineering. I never wanted to be like her so I worked at being sweet and selfless. I've been to your Personality seminars and I think my mother was the Powerful Choleric personality—angry, bossy, and domineering. My father was Phlegmatic—peaceful, quiet, and ready to go to any lengths to avoid conflict. I saw him as weak and my mother as strong. I felt my mother was the problem. Didn't she push everyone around? Didn't Dad and I have to escape into work

47

and school to keep away from her? Although I could identify with the various personalities, I didn't really understand how they worked. I determined not to be like my mother when I grew up. I decided to change and become the dear, sweet, submissive type I'd heard about in church. Now I think I've become a phony. Can you help me?

Phony in Phoenix

Dear Phony:

Some of us grew up in homes where we didn't like the balance of power and vowed when we got married things would be different. But how many of us have repeated our family's mistakes without even realizing what we were doing? It seems that's what you've done, and now it's time to stop pretending to be someone you're not. Be real. Be yourself.

Phony's real name was Margaret, and I began to work with her on the telephone. I explained to her that when we try to shift personality types and pretend to be something we aren't, we cross up God's plan for us and we actually start working at odds with what we were created to be. Ultimately this can end up causing not only personality problems, but social and emotional troubles and even physical pain. I've never met a truly happy woman who was functioning outside of her birth personality. Rather than remake herself, Margaret should have analyzed her mother's weaknesses. Then she would have seen how much her father's reserved personality caused her mother's extremes, and she could have determined to avoid the pitfalls herself.

Instead, Margaret watched TV, pretending to be the lead in each show, and aimed to have a marriage like the one in *Father Knows Best*. She told me, "In my teens I formed ideas of what kind of marriage I wanted. It certainly wasn't going to be like my parents' marriage. I didn't want to be bossy like Mother or have a weak husband like my father. I would seek out the opposite!"

And she did! Once Margaret started playing the demure heroine role, she attracted a strong Choleric man who was certainly in control of himself and soon of her. For many years she played her part well, covering up her frustrations and depression by doing and saying all the right things. In spite of her positive pretending, however, Margaret knew her marriage was failing when she first wrote to me.

She recalled, "The day I realized I was being my dad and I had married my mother was a shocker! But once I could see the source of the problem, the healing began."

It was at this point that Margaret came to CLASS and began to study the Personalities and apply the knowledge to her situation. She started to pray that the Lord would restore those lost years of confused identity and make her a genuine person. Her husband was stunned when his submissive wife began offering opinions, but he did begin to notice her in a new and positive way. To change a long-term trend in marriage is not easy, but Margaret knew it was worth working for. She said, "It was a long ten years, which included several sessions of CLASS, Southern California women's retreats, a day of healing prayer, and almost a divorce, but our power structure and roles eventually became much more balanced. My husband even told the counselor that he likes me 'brassy'!"

Margaret's being brassy isn't actually what he likes, but that Margaret is finally *real.* No one likes to live with a phony, even if he or she isn't discerning enough to recognize the disguise.

Margaret has worked prayerfully and with outside help to become her true Sanguine and Choleric self, to be fun-loving and humorous and to be able to state her feelings clearly, firmly, and lovingly. I have personally been involved in the changes and have seen the spiritual and emotional growth as Margaret has determined to be real.

Uncovering Deception

While *denial* is often an unconscious act of covering up the truth, and *pretending* is a conscious act of believing things are better than they really are, *deception* is a plot to fool and trick ourselves and others or prevent the truth from being known. Initially we deceive only ourselves, but after a while we extend the cover-up to others. Remember when, as children, we told a white lie to a friend and then had to continue lying to keep the first lie secure? Remember **49** how confusing it became and how we ultimately were caught in our own story? It's like the lines in that classic poem: "Oh what a tangled web we weave, when first we practice to deceive!"[3]

Dear Florence:

Why do some supposedly good women lie? My friend's husband is a heavy drinker and sometimes I see him stagger, but when I ask her, she says he has poor balance. Others have tried to talk to her about him and she just denies any problems. It's like she looks the other way and pretends he's okay.

Why Lie in White Plains

Dear Why Lie:

Your friend may have denied her husband's problems at first, then pretended things were better than they were, and then moved on to weave a web of deceptions for herself and others. Many well-meaning women are living a lie today and hoping no one will find out. So many of the women who come to me start with the sentence, "I've never told this to anyone before." After that comes an assortment of confessions: "I was abused as a child." "My son is on drugs." "My husband's a church elder but he beats me." "He's a closet alcoholic." "He's been having a series of affairs." "He's a compulsive gambler." "He's gay!"

No normal woman sets out to be a liar, but in all these cases the woman has been living a lie. She didn't mean to or want to, but she got caught in a tangled web of deception. Many of these women believe if they bring the truth out in the open they will be ostracized from the Christian community. In some cases, they are right. Yet keeping the truth hidden is causing them to have headaches, stomach upsets, or nervous exhaustion, to overeat, and often to withdraw from any meaningful relationships. When we are living in a deceptive environment, it is as if we are constantly onstage in a theatrical production twenty-four hours a day with no intermission. We are worn out.

Perhaps you could approach your friend and tell her you understand why she doesn't open up with you. Share some example from your own life where you hid something from others. Let her know you want to help her and won't tell anyone else. Let her know she doesn't need to live this way any longer. No matter what our problems are, there are others who have similar burdens who will understand. There are support groups and twelve-step programs for almost every type of emotional or addictive situation imaginable. Help her to see that the first step is always to recognize we have a problem and want to do something about it, humanly and prayerfully.

Show her that when we continue to *deny* addictions or abuse, *pretend* things will right themselves tomorrow, and *deceive* ourselves and others, we become one of those dysfunctional people we always believed lived in someone else's neighborhood.

Dysfunction

Dear Florence:

Are there any normal people left? It seems everybody is at least a little bit peculiar!

Normal Nancy

Dear Normal:

I once saw a cartoon that showed an auditorium with a banner that said "National Convention for Children of Normal Parents." There was only one child in the audience! The cartoon wouldn't be convicting if it did not represent the current thinking that nobody is normal anymore. But if we are all somewhat dysfunctional, does that include you and me?

According to the *New York Times,* "Americans participated in an estimated 100 million therapy sessions with licensed practitioners in the year ending June, 1992, and paid approximately $8.1 billion, not counting prescription drugs, to relieve this national despair."[4]

One hundred million therapy sessions. That seems like enough to take in all of us, yet the writer points out this does not include those who went to pastors, lay counselors, physicians, or friends for advice or those who stayed home and read books on codependency and mental health. The total doesn't even pretend to include Christian books and seminars.

51

If we as a nation are in such a bad emotional condition and we as Christians are to be examples for the rest, then we had better check ourselves out. Are we living in *denial* of our pain, *pretending* we are happy Christians, *deceiving* ourselves and others?

In the good old days we had "normal" standards and values. We all believed the Bible, followed the Golden Rule, and recognized the Ten Commandments. But in today's permissive society normal isn't normal anymore. We've all been told to do our own thing (even by some well meaning pastors and Christian leaders) and that has produced chaos. Stay "normal" yourself, and pray for the others.

When Submission Becomes Codependency

Dear Florence:

What does it mean to be submissive? Some women I know are so sweet it's sickening. Either I'm off base or they've been misinformed.

Not Sweet in Summerville

Dear Not Sweet:

Some of us Christian women are so steeped in the need to be submissive that we make our husbands into fathers who must take care of us. We appear to be the most devout of wives, worshiping our husbands. I had a friend Gina who was like that. She adored her husband and praised his every move. "Isn't he handsome?" she'd ask, and we all had to say, "He's the handsomest man we've ever met."

"Isn't he wonderful, intelligent, spiritual?" Yes, yes, yes. When together at social functions, Gina would cling to Daryl's arm and coo at his every word. While the rest of the women were in the kitchen, Gina would be with Daryl and the men, who frankly wished she'd buzz off.

She never made even the tiniest decision without calling Daryl at work. She didn't seem able to plug in the coffeepot without his instruction. When he was out of town on business, Gina was a wreck; often she got physically sick awaiting his return. Gina was without a doubt the most submissive woman in the church—and proud of it.

Imagine her total shock on the day when she was kissing Daryl good-bye and clinging to him and he shoved her away. "I'm so sick of your whining all over me," he snarled at her. "When are you going to grow up and be a real woman?" With that he slammed the door and drove off to work.

"What am I doing wrong?" she cried to me over the phone. "You know what a good wife I've been. I've put him first in everything."

What was wrong here? Gina had a distorted view of submission and when I talked to Daryl he said he felt suffocated by this child-wife who couldn't move without his direction or talk without his words. It took a time of separation and counseling to help Gina grow up and become a responsible adult, one who could think through a problem, come up with a rational decision, and take charge of her life. We don't need to be whiny sweet to be submissive.

When submission becomes a codependent relationship, we women may be drowning our husbands. We need to be polite and aim to please but also use our heads and be responsible for our lives.

Kay had a similar problem. She prided herself on being the submissive wife. She worried over every little thing and always looked to Sam to fix whatever was wrong. He was strong and capable and always made things better when times got tough. He felt this was his responsibility as the head of the house. Sam was a self-employed builder and the picture of physical health and strength until he turned forty-nine and began to experience chest pains. After several tests he learned the main artery to his heart was more than 95 percent blocked. The doctors did three angioplasties that didn't hold and eventually tried experimental surgery not yet approved by governmental agencies.

As Kay sat alone in the motel near the hospital, she read 1 Peter and was struck with the thought of being called to suffer with and glorify Christ. Kay feared her husband would die, and she wondered how she could ever function without him, let alone be used to glorify Christ in her suffering.

Kay tells what happened next:

Alone in my motel room I cried out to God, "I'm afraid, God! Don't let Sam die. I love him; I need him!" I remembered the theme of 1 Peter. I didn't like having to suffer with and glorify Christ. But then I felt God telling me to rest in His arms, put my trust totally in Him, and He would do the glorifying through me. I realized I had not been the submissive little wife; I had been the codependent little wife. I needed to put God first. I could trust Him and find comfort in His arms. Submission to God comes first; submission to one another under the headship of Christ follows.

My husband is doing very well physically now, but our lives have changed. You see, the more I depend on God the more freedom it gives my husband to not have to always make things better for me. When I find myself slipping back into putting Sam first, I remind myself that I can rest in my Savior's arms, that He is worthy of my total submission to Him. I am working to "grow up" in Christ.

Kay has become a real person. She has taken control of her life and is no longer living it through Sam. They are partners in marriage, and Sam is relieved of the unreasonable responsibility Kay had placed on him in the guise of being a submissive wife.

Kay is now a staff minister to women in her church, teaching them to grow up, to be submissive to the Lord Jesus Christ, and to not be codependent on their husbands.

Dear Florence:

I teach women's classes in my church and the women all seem to be victims of something. Do you have a checklist I could use as a framework to get to the heart of their problems? We women need to be the emotional cords that hold our homes together and yet many of these women seem immature and are avoiding the truth. Help me to help them.

Trying in Toledo

Dear Trying:

Thank you for taking time to be a mature model for these women. There are so many today who have had no godly role models to follow and who will grow from your training. I'm printing a list of questions for you that will provide a basis for truthful self-evaluation.

There is enough information in this list to keep your discussions going for weeks. First have the women jot down their answers on their own papers and then review their opinions.

Self-Analysis Quiz

	Yes	No
1. Do you feel like you are living in a dysfunctional situation?		
2. Does one person control the rest of your family?		
3. Is there one person whom everyone's afraid of?		
4. Is there one person who causes problems for the others?		
5. Are you unhappy when you are with one certain person?		
6. Are you more yourself when you are apart from this person?		
7. Are you restricted in your social life by the demands at home?		
8. Do you sometimes feel like a prisoner in your own home?		
9. Have you been denying your emotional pain and problems?		
10. Do you often say, "Well, others have it worse than I do"?		
11. Are you afraid of someone's angry outbursts? of being beaten? of retaliation?		
12. Are there alcohol or drug problems in your home?		
13. Are you pretending things are better than they are?		
14. Are you accepting abuse by hoping it will stop tomorrow?		
15. Is your optimism really self-deception?		
16. Do you think submission means you have no rights?		

17. Do you think that enduring abuse is suffering for Jesus? ____ ____
18. Do you think Christians should pretend to be happy no matter how they feel? ____ ____
19. Do you rationalize and make excuses for the behavior of your family members? ____ ____
20. Would you admit to yourself that your household is out of control at the moment? ____ ____
21. Are you prevented from getting the health care you need? ____ ____
22. Are you kept ignorant of family finances? ____ ____
23. Do you sometimes feel there's just no hope? ____ ____
24. If no one held you accountable, would you pack up and leave tomorrow? ____ ____
25. Do you feel tangled in a web of deception that you can't begin to untie? ____ ____

For those whose emotions have been triggered by these questions, perhaps you need to think over your situation. Are you being oppressed or abused? Do you think being a doormat is what submission means? Have you been denying difficult problems?

If you've been living a lie, even though it's not your fault, it's time to wake up to the reality around you and take steps to get beyond and above your situation. There is hope. You don't have to be a victim of circumstances any longer. You *can* take charge of your life.

Denial (refusing to acknowledge the past)
plus
Pretending (thinking the future will automatically get better)
plus
Deception (hiding the truth in the present)
equals
Dysfunction (abnormal behavior)

Untangling the Web of Denial, Pretending, Deception, and Dysfunction

No matter what your problems may be, this book is intended to help you get in touch with reality, quit pretending, and face the facts. Until we women take charge of our lives, we can't establish meaningful relationships with anyone.

I met with one couple who pretended their problems weren't all that bad. When I got around to asking some specific questions, the wife asked, "Would it be all right if he left the room for a while?" He agreed to go, and after he'd shut the door she explained, "I had to get him out of here because everything I've told you so far is a lie." She then poured out a story of a lifetime of deception including a sexual relationship with her father, affairs during her marriage, and a Christian daughter who was living with an abusive man. This last problem bothered her the most and she was working hard to keep it from the church in hopes her fellow Christians would never know her perfect family wasn't perfect. No wonder this lady was overweight, a compulsive talker, exhausted, and a nervous wreck. She was working so hard to conceal the truth that her tangled web was in knots.

How about your life? Is it time for you to unravel some of the knots in your past and present so you can get control of your life in the future? Look at the chart in the appendix comparing three prominent views of current issues affecting Christian women. Which view represents the way you look at potential dysfunctions in your life or your family? Is yours the world view, the balanced Christian view, or the legalistic view?

You don't want to be one of those dysfunctional people. You want to be in charge of your life.

four

Where, Oh Where,
Have All the Good *Husbands Gone?*

I often conduct informal surveys of CLASS participants and other groups of women so I can stay current on women's experiences and attitudes on modern issues. During one recent survey, a group of exemplary Christian women from many different denominations wrote about how blessed they were and how happy they felt. They seemed to be content with their lives. But when they were questioned more closely, one on one, they told different stories. Some admitted they had poor marriages, some were being emotionally abused, some had financial problems, some felt put down by their husbands or by men at work or in the church, and some thought other Christians were judging them. When asked why they had not written this on the survey, they said that since they were Christians they couldn't let themselves put any negatives in writing. Someone might figure out who they were and think they weren't spiritual enough, they said.

Such surveys have taught me that Christian women tell the truth less often than people of the world. It's not that we lie, exactly; it's that we feel we are hurting the cause of Christ if we give the facts of our lives as they really are. Not only do we cover up our feelings, but we make excuses for our husband's abusive behavior. Until we face the truth we can't improve our lives.

The stories in this chapter are those of a number of women who have come to me with unusual problems. These are women who, like those in the survey mentioned earlier, would have said they were joyful Christians, not because they *were,* but because that is what they felt they were *supposed* to be. Women like Helen, who reported her husband's continuous insults and occasional physical abuse: "He beat me black and blue. But he's really a nice man and I know he doesn't mean to. I wouldn't want you to think negatively about him." It doesn't matter if he means well. If he's doing this, he is not a nice man! Stop apologizing and face the truth. Until we are honest and look at our problems without denial, we are helpless to act upon them. And we won't be any better off ten years from now. So let's face it today!

These stories are fascinating when they are not our stories; yet as we think about them, there may be a little of these women in each of us or in some of our friends. Let's examine our lives honestly as we look at theirs.

The Bigamist

Cynthia had a master's degree in English literature. Her husband handled everything and gave her an allowance that was more than adequate. She had no checking account or credit cards but always had enough cash. Cynthia had no idea where the money came from or how much there was in reserve. She was even a little hazy on what Al actually did for a living. He said he had an importing business and had to go out of town frequently. As the children grew up, he occasionally missed important holidays, but as long as the money was there, Cynthia didn't mind, and she made excuses for his absence.

Whenever her church had a fund-raiser, Al gave a large contribution even though he rarely had time to go. Sundays were particularly busy days for Al; he always seemed to have emergency calls from the office that day that required him to go in to work. Cynthia's friends envied her comfortable lifestyle even though it was a little lonely.

When Al, was about forty he came home from having a physical and said he had been proclaimed impotent. This surprised Cynthia because he had not seemed to have any sexual problems before the exam. From that time on, though, he seemed embarrassed to sleep with her and "sacrificed" by moving into another bedroom.

One day Cynthia's thirteen-year-old daughter Jody came home from school and told Cynthia about this new girl in class who looked just like her. The child seemed disturbed about it, but Cynthia passed it off as a coincidence until Jody brought the girl home with her. The resemblance was uncanny and un-Christian thoughts went through Cynthia's mind. She chastised herself for even thinking that Al could have somehow fathered this child, but she surely did look like him and Jody. She wanted to ask him about it, but he hated to be questioned about anything. She did ask the child where she lived and found it was only a few streets away. Cynthia started driving by the house frequently—and one Sunday when Al was supposedly at the office handling another emergency call, she saw his car in the driveway.

Cynthia felt sick to her stomach; she didn't know what to do. She drove home and went straight to his desk. The first thing she found was two sets of checkbooks. One set was labeled A, the other B, and neither was imprinted with an address. A had carbons of checks to pay her mortgage and bills, and B had similar checks made out to a different mortgage company. She could hardly wait until Monday to call the mortgage company and check the address of the second mortgage. Sure enough, it was for the other woman's house!

When Al came home Monday night, he found Cynthia and their pastor waiting for him. When they confronted him, he confessed to leading a dual life and having another wife and family for fifteen years. The other family had been in another state, but it had been too inconvenient for Al, so he had brought them closer. Somehow he never thought they'd find each other.

When Cynthia told me this fascinating story, she was divorcing Al, who had chosen to stay with Lady B and her young family. Cynthia kept as quiet about it as possible to save her children from shame; she plans to move away at the end of the school year. **61**

"Was I ever naive!" Cynthia said. "I didn't want to question where he was on holidays and Sundays. I didn't know anything about our money. It turned out the life insurance was in her name, and although I didn't know it, I'd had no health insurance for two years."

Why didn't Cynthia ask any questions?

One reason was her basic trust in mankind, which is a positive trait in all of us. Another was that she was living well and had no obvious clues about Al's hidden life. It's a lot easier to look the other way when you're not hungry. Cynthia would have known earlier about Al's deceitfulness if she'd spot-checked his Sundays in the office or his nights in distant hotels.

When Al proclaimed himself impotent at forty, Cynthia just accepted it as a medical fact. She didn't ask the doctor's name or suggest they go see him together for further diagnosis and treatment. In truth, there was no doctor's visit at all; but Cynthia didn't even ask, making Al's lack of sexual interest in her a lot easier to excuse.

Because Cynthia never questioned his finances or asked to be shown the insurance policy, Al was able to leave the "paper trail" right under her nose in his desk at home.

Their children are not only humiliated and angry at Al, but they're also furious at Cynthia for her years of blind indifference. "How could you be so stupid?" they asked. But Cynthia wasn't stupid. She just didn't ask any questions.

Probably none of you have a husband who's a bigamist, but would you really know if you did? Do you have access to all of the insurance policies, checkbooks, investments, and the will? Do you accept his absences without checking? Are there gaps in his life that don't add up? If this is your situation, it's time to wake up!

The Workaholic

Jennifer described how hard her husband worked: "Poor man. He doesn't get home until two in the morning and he's off again at seven." Since she had brought up the subject, I asked if she had ever checked at midnight to make sure he was at the office.

"Oh no! I wouldn't do that," she gasped. "He told me that a real Christian wife is trusting and has faith in her husband. He's really big on trust."

I didn't want to discourage her, but I don't know many men who can work that hard for long. One day Jennifer called to say, "He's divorcing me. He wasn't working after all."

The Stripper

Several times Martha wondered why her doctor husband didn't answer his page when she tried to reach him. He always had excuses of emergencies that had come up, but somehow his words didn't ring true. One day he turned on her and snapped, "Don't ever try to check on me again. What I do is none of your business."

His reaction frightened her, but it also made her more determined to find out where he was in these missing hours. She hired a detective and fully expected to find her husband was having an affair. She was dumbfounded when the detective came back with pictures of her fine Christian husband coming out of a huge cake and doing striptease shows at women's parties. He had a post office box and ran ads in the personal columns. Clients looking for such entertainment would write to the box number, then he would call and set up an appointment. He was paid in cash and no one ever knew his name.

The Rapist

Ronda wrote to me about the shock in her life when her husband's deceptions were brought to light:

Eleven years ago my marriage was dealt a deadly blow. My husband of seven years was arrested for the kidnapping and rape of a sixteen-year-old in the small South Texas town where we were living. It turned out he was also deeply enmeshed in burglary, drugs, and alcohol. I was to discover that he was in fact a serial rapist. He had forsaken the God he once knew and loved. His double life, expertly hidden behind a wall of silence and depression, came as a great shock to me and my children. The morning after his arrest,

63

the police searched our home. It was as if I were standing naked before a roomful of strangers. Our lives were laid bare before them. What little self-esteem I had was destroyed that day.

Ronda's husband was sentenced to thirty years in a state penitentiary, and she found herself a broken, devastated mother of two. There was no time to sit around and feel sorry for herself, no money for counseling, and few friends left to give her support:

> I found myself at the breaking point, desperate before God for a complete healing. I discovered that I had stuffed the closet of my heart with package after package of pain. The closet was full, and I could no longer shut the door and ignore it. I began rummaging through, sorting and tossing and making order out of my life once more. Through it all, as difficult as it has been, God has begun to do a work in my life. My inner strength has grown along with my character, compassion, and faith. God, who was the beloved Guardian of my childhood, has once again become Lord of my life.
>
> I watched a log burn in a fireplace one night, and I wept. "That's how my life is, Lord," I whispered. "It's been destroyed, and I'm useless." That greatest of all counselors listened, let me cry, and then soothed my spirit. Then He reminded me of Isaiah 61:3, "To appoint unto them that mourn . . . to give unto them beauty for ashes, the oil of joy for mourning, the garment of praise for the spirit of heaviness, that they might be called trees of righteousness, the planting of the Lord, that he might be glorified."
>
> So I brought to God a rusty old bucket, filled with the ashes of my life, and He has begun to turn them into a "planting, that He might be glorified." And I stand in awe at the wonder of such a God and am humbled that He could love and care for me.

In the process of healing, Ronda has come to CLASS to learn how she can help other women see the signs before it's too late. She feels the Lord leading her to speak out even more; she has been on *Sally Jessy Raphael, Inside Edition,* and *Hard Copy* and is the subject of Kevin Flynn's book, *The Unmasking: Married to a Rapist.* She is thrilled when she can put the arms of Jesus around one hurting lady and give her a spark of hope.

The Sexual Deviate

Candy was married at an early age to a young man who won her over by his charm and good looks. He swept her off her feet, just as Prince Charming was supposed to do. However, her dream was severely shattered on her wedding night when Candy was forcibly raped by her husband and thrown out of their honeymoon cottage naked, an act he considered funny. Candy was humiliated and devastated. She should have been on her way to the nearest police station or at the very least a bus station for a ticket home, but Candy wanted to live "happily ever after," and she convinced herself she could make it work.

And she did work at it—for twenty-two long years. During her deteriorating marriage she was expected to participate in skinny-dipping parties, nudist camps, hot-tub clubs, and X-rated movies—all aimed at improving her sexual performance. Candy set out to be the sexiest girl at these events in order to keep her philandering husband interested. But her efforts were unsuccessful. Not only did he have numerous affairs and encounters with other women, but he sexually abused his own daughters.

When Candy finally started saying no to her husband's demands, he became violent. Candy finally took the girls and left, twenty-two years too late.

Because of Candy's denial of her husband's perverse behavior for so many years, she has had to face far greater consequences than if she had faced it from the beginning. Sadly, her daughters, innocent victims, have had to endure abuse that is hard to undo, even with Christian counseling.

Often our fear of the unknown causes us to put up with behavior that should never be tolerated. Sometimes it is the dread of facing a failed relationship and the judgment of others that causes us to stay in marriages filled with violence or perversions. Too many times it's not being able to make it financially that figures into our reasons for hanging on when we should run the other way.

Candy didn't want to face the death of her dream for a happily-ever-after life. But she finally put her trust in the right Prince—Jesus—and had the courage to get help for herself and her girls. **65**

Candy now ministers to others who have been through similar situations. She has been a guest on many radio programs and shares her story and insights into finding victory in Jesus over sexual, emotional, and physical abuse.

The Slave Driver

Sarah was a student nurse when she started dating Reza. After Sarah's fiancé was killed in Vietnam, her friends had introduced her to Reza. When Reza wined and dined Sarah, the overt attention was extremely flattering, and Sarah was very vulnerable.

Their dates turned to talk about marriage, and they started looking at homes and rings. They decided to get married in Las Vegas and then visit his homeland for a traditional Arabian ceremony.

As the time drew closer to their marriage date, Reza said he would buy her a "huge diamond ring" in Iraq because he could get it there much cheaper. He postponed buying the home they had chosen because, he said, he couldn't see letting it sit idle while they honeymooned in Iraq.

The day they arrived in Las Vegas, Reza decided to visit the casinos before finding a chapel to have the wedding ceremony. He gave Sarah a few dollars and told her to enjoy the slot machines while he went to the gambling tables. When she asked when they were going to get married, he kept saying "later, later." Since later became still later, Reza dropped Sarah off at a motel so she could rest; he continued to gamble.

When Reza returned the next morning, Sarah was having doubts whether she should go ahead with the wedding. When she voiced her doubts to him, he threatened to abandon her on the streets of Las Vegas if she didn't comply. She decided that marrying Reza seemed better than being left alone. If she'd only known!

Fortunately for Sarah, Reza decided the Mideast was too full of conflict to return there. Instead, they settled in an apartment. Still, life became increasingly difficult for her. Sarah was never again allowed to go with him to look for a new home, and after a while Reza lost interest in looking and invested the money in his business. Sarah was never allowed to see the checkbook or inquire about where the money was going.

Reza kept Sarah away from people, even making her stay in the back room of his business doing menial tasks while he dealt with customers. Sarah was not allowed to go to the grocery store until she refused to cook because her cupboards were bare. When he did allow her to make a trip anywhere, he accompanied her and told her to keep her eyes down and not to look at any men. She had to use a checkout line that was operated by a woman.

Reza insisted that Sarah prove her value and worthiness as his wife by conceiving, and he demanded that she find a woman doctor to treat her during the pregnancy because no other man should be allowed to see her body.

Sarah became more and more unhappy and depressed, but she stayed with him and had two more children. As Reza became both physically and mentally abusive, Sarah feared for her life. He slept with a gun under his pillow and told her that if she ever left him, he would hunt her down and kill her. He continually accused her of having affairs if she ever went anywhere without him. She had to obey his every whim; Reza became the slave driver and Sarah the menial slave.

On trips in the car, he would leave Sarah and their three children in the parking lot in the heat and go into the restaurant to eat alone. On occasions when they were invited to come along, Sarah had to share a meal with the three children and was not allowed to order anything to drink. He would humiliate her by aggressively flirting with the waitresses and insulting her in front of them.

After eleven years of an abusive marriage, Sarah decided she had to leave. The threat of death didn't sound as bad as the thought of having to live like a slave forever.

Sarah and her children were held captive by a deceptive man who had no intention of being a good husband or father. His only concern and thoughts were for himself and for his own needs. Is anyone holding your life captive to fill his own needs? If so, perhaps it's time for you to decide, as Sarah did, that things need to **67** change. I hope your situation is not this desperate, but you may need to instigate some changes to make your relationships healthy.

All of the women whose stories I've shared here—Cynthia, Jennifer, Martha, Ronda, Candy, and Sarah—are Christians. Each got married with the best of intentions, and each trusted her husband too much.

We don't need to turn ourselves into suspicious, vicious women who keep our husbands under surveillance, but we do need to alert our minds to possible problems. We need to know it's not bad to want financial information or to want our husbands to account for large gaps of missing time. In each of the previous cases the situation was so far gone before it was recognized that there was little chance of redemption. Nancy's story is different.

The Philanderer

Nancy Norton's husband always kept in touch with her when he was on the road, but one day as he left he said he wasn't sure where he'd be staying that week. This sounded odd to her and made her wonder. She called his office and asked the secretary to give her the name of the hotel since he had forgotten to tell her. She called the hotel that night and asked for Mr. and Mrs. Norton. A woman answered the phone in the room. Nancy, in a burst of quick, creative thinking said, "This is the front desk. When will you and Mr. Norton be checking out?" The female voice answered, "On Thursday."

"Thank you so much, Mrs. Norton," the real Mrs. Norton said.

The next afternoon Nancy got in her car and drove the many hours to the hotel. She sat in a corner of the lobby, somewhat hidden. At dinner time the elevator opened and out stepped her husband and a sweet young thing. She waited until they were seated in the dining room and then slipped into the booth beside them.

"What a surprise to find you here," she chirped cheerfully.

She told me later that the look on their faces was worth the trip. From that point on, Nancy traveled with him as much as possible and they kept in close touch. While their marriage was far from ideal, they were able to put their life back together because Nancy nipped the affair in the bud and was willing to forgive.

Red Flags

Dear Florence:

I don't want to be overly suspicious of my husband or make him think I don't trust him, but sometimes I wonder. Can you give me a list of reasonable things I should watch out for, a list of warnings perhaps?

Slightly Suspicious

Dear Slightly:

In my experience I rarely find women who are overly suspicious, although there are some. But I frequently talk with those who did not notice the obvious red flags waving before them.

What are some reasonable questions to ask? What should you be alert to in your marriage relationship? When any of the following symptoms are evident, it's time to do a reality check.

1. **Expenditures of money that are unexplainable.** Obviously, if you have nothing to do with the family finances, you have no way to see discrepancies before it's too late, but you should have at least a basic knowledge of what comes in and what goes out.
2. **Excessive amounts of time spent at work or other unaccounted-for spans of time.** Many of us work more than the forty-hour week, but if your mate is working every night for more than emergencies, volunteer to go in and help. If he refuses to let you join him or check up on him, you know you are in trouble.
3. **Disinterest in family functions.** If a man who has enjoyed his children no longer wants to be with them or refuses to go to their programs, and if he has urgent business on holidays and weekends, you had better check up on him.
4. **Gaps in accountability and discrepancies in stories.** If you call and he's always out to lunch or not where he said he'd be, you have a right to ask. Don't become his mother, but ask

when you feel in your spirit that his excuses don't make sense. And if his stories don't add up, do some checking.

5. **Secretive behavior.** If he seems to be nervous when you ask where he's going or gets defensive when you question him or gives you lectures on trust, watch out!

6. **Sudden changes in looks and activities.** If he has a new desire to exercise, joins a co-ed health club, buys silk underwear, and starts test-driving red Corvettes, you may be in trouble.

7. **Lack of communication.** If he withdraws and refuses to talk about anything but the most trivial matters ("What's for dinner?" or "Have you seen my brown argyle socks?") you have to start wondering if his mind is focused on something or someone else.

8. **No interest in sex.** Some women take this as a relief and not a warning sign.

9. **Mysterious phone calls.** If there are suspicious messages or if he talks for long periods of time off in another room with the door shut and gets upset if you pick up the phone, watch out!

Many women I counsel have lived through all of these symptoms and yet have not confronted the problem. Instead they live in hope that it will all go away. They don't realize that the sooner the facts are faced the better chance there is of recovery and restoration. The longer unusual behavior is allowed to progress, the sooner it becomes a habit that is extremely difficult to break.

Don't get depressed if you realize you need to face some of these issues. The good news is that if you will take these steps to take charge, you *can* begin to have a new and happier life!

PART *two*

CLAIMING GOD'S BEST FOR YOUR FUTURE

Managing the Money

When I was growing up women didn't need to know anything about money. We expected our husbands to earn and control the money and give us what we needed to run the household. But in these difficult times, we must understand things we never thought we'd have to handle. Father may know best, but what if he's not around? What if he's dead or divorced? What if he's injured on the job? What if he's never been good with money? We cannot hide from responsibility or turn our heads in the other direction.

Personality and Money

Dear Florence:

My husband and I are new Christians and we want to do this right. The people at our church say the men must take charge of the money and the women should just trust them. My husband's never handled money before. What should we do?

Trusting in Texas   **73**

Dear Trusting:

Handling money is not a male-only ability. God did not prohibit women from business ventures. Lydia sold purple, Philip's daughters were out on the road as traveling evangelists, and even the Proverbs 31 woman was buying and selling property.

We are each born with certain talents. The question is not whether a male or female is best at handling money, but which personality can do the best job. Not all men have a feel for finances and not all women have a fear of figures.

No matter how little or how much our families have, we want to use it wisely. To do this most effectively, it is helpful to know the personalities of all family members so we can understand their differences.

Before Fred and I understood personality strengths and weaknesses, we wondered why we had one child who analyzed her allowance and apportioned it correctly and one who spent it foolishly and had no money for lunch on Friday. Hadn't we taught them both in the same way? Hadn't they each received the amount they needed?

When we identified the family members' individual personalities, we understood their financial characteristics too. If you are good at handling the money and both you and your husband are pleased by that arrangement, keep it up. Don't fix what's not broken.

Dear Florence:

In our family we are all mixed up on money. We are arguing about what we spend and we can't agree. My husband says he must be right because he's the man. Can you explain why we see things so differently?

Mixed Up in Minneapolis

Dear Mixed Up:

Understanding the Personalities and their differences will help you see why you are all disagreeing. The Popular Sanguine loves money and the things it will buy. Sanguines tend to be lustful after possessions and greedy to have more of everything than their friends. Since their basic desire is to have fun, money seems to guarantee a ticket to happiness. Sanguines have little thought for tomorrow, and the idea of a budget or discipline never enters their heads. They have little natural interest in numbers and balancing checkbooks is a chore to be postponed.

A Sanguine husband will need some kind of assistance in handling finances or the family may be bankrupt before anyone knows what's going on. Sanguines are so desperate for people to love and admire them that they will do whatever it takes to be the good guy in any situation. Sanguines' combination of natural generosity and poor grasp of figures causes them to go quickly into debt. When checks start to bounce they are genuinely surprised—and their mates are furious. "Didn't you know you didn't have anything in the checking account?" they rage.

"No—I guess I forgot to write in the amounts."

"I can't believe you are so stupid!"

Since the Sanguines crave praise, criticism from their mates so depresses them that they go shopping to cheer themselves up. And the cycle starts again.

Sanguines love excitement and want to go on every outing or vacation that comes along regardless of cost. They will gladly go into debt for the pursuit of pleasure and frequently live today off of what they hope to earn tomorrow. They buy equipment for every sport or hobby before they know if they even like it or can do it. If they're going to take up golf, they'll buy the best clubs available. If they plan to take piano lessons, they'll purchase a piano.

Judy told me her Sanguine husband decided to take up woodworking during their long Canadian winter. She bought him a little kit in a hobby shop and he began to carve wooden figures. He had such fun that he decided to get better equipment; soon he had the best money could buy. "He could have competed with Michelangelo!" Judy said in disgust. Typically, when spring came his interest left with the daffodils. He hasn't carved since.

Opposite of the spending Sanguine is the meticulous Melancholy, who watches over every cent like a hawk. Money is doled out carefully, and an accounting must be made of every expenditure. **75**

Melancholies love figures, charts, graphs, and budgets. They can stare at ledger books for hours. They find errors in everyone else's work, causing others to refuse to work with them. ("If that's the way you're going to be, you can do it yourself.") They have high standards, and when the rest of the family bounces along, blithely indifferent, Melancholies become depressed. "Am I the only one who cares?" they fume. "This whole family is like a kindergarten."

Melancholies rarely get into financial problems on their own; if they do buy over their heads, it's not for a trivial pleasure but a superior machine or computer that will enhance their pursuit of perfection. Sometimes they spend so much time analyzing all the different products, reading *Consumer Reports,* and asking for other people's opinions that the item is outdated by the time they've chosen the right model.

It is easy to see why the frivolous, fun-loving Sanguine loses patience with the nit-picking Melancholy. Ideally, since this pair usually gets married, the Melancholy should keep the books but not be fanatical about it. The Sanguine needs to have some "fun money" that doesn't need to be accounted for but also needs to work on curbing his or her spending habits. The Sanguine can loosen up the Melancholy and the Melancholy can rein in the Sanguine but only if they understand their differences and communicate on the subject without hostility.

For the Powerful Choleric money spells success. Cholerics don't spend foolishly nor do they sit around and meditate over it. Money is a tool, a bargaining chip. Cholerics want to be thought of as successful and they will use money to impress others with how well they have done in life. Usually they are the movers and shakers, but they are not beyond manipulating others to achieve their own goals. They believe that the end justifies the means. Others see them as cold and calculating, but they feel they are doing what any person with intelligence would choose.

Cholerics love challenges, and they seem to do the impossible. It just takes a little longer. The words "it can't be done" move them into action. "I'll show them," they mumble under their breath.

Because of their need to be heroes they sometimes take risks that lead to financial ruin, but even then they find ways to borrow and start over again. They have such confidence in their ability that events that devastate their mate are only a bump in the road for them. They can usually see the big picture and move on toward it.

Their aggressive attitude toward success is frustrating to a more conservative mate who tries in vain to tone them down, only to see them throw caution to the wind and enter into a new and dangerous business opportunity. One of Cholerics' biggest weaknesses is to think they don't have any! They rarely seek counsel or listen to anyone with a different opinion. Their mate tries in vain to get them to talk to the banker or Uncle Harry before jumping into a new venture, but they refuse. "Why should I listen to him when I know what I'm going to do anyway?"

When Cholerics are successful, they can be great achievers and provide a lavish lifestyle, but all too often they keep their family hanging over a cliff for so long that even the ravine below looks better than living on the edge.

The conservative Phlegmatic is often married to the daring Choleric, and their life together is chaotic. The Phlegmatic, whose aim is to keep peace and avoid problems, can't stand the adventurous mate and yet can't seem to deal with impending disaster. After a few protests, the Phlegmatic retreats and pretends not to care. "Let the chips fall where they may."

Left to themselves the Phlegmatics are dependable and responsible with money and want to avoid controversy at all costs. They don't see problems coming as the Melancholy does, they aren't daring as the Cholerics, and they don't throw money around like the Sanguines. They'd really be happy if they didn't have to look at money problems at all.

Phlegmatics' weakness with money is that they are trusting of others and can't say no to those who appear to be in need. Even though Phlegmatics tend to be stingy with themselves, they easily fall prey to the sob story of a friend and give graciously without investigating the probability of return. When the mate finds they have once again been a soft touch without discussing it, he or she gets furious and rants and raves. "How could you do this to me?" This attack causes the peace-loving Phlegmatic to retreat, build a defensive wall, and vow never to be nice to anyone again. Phlegmatics need to be needed and because their mate usually can function adequately without them, they seek people who need them outside of the family, reopening the possibility of financial victimization.

The Phlegmatic usually doesn't make decisions quickly. This caution is good in questionable investments but annoying when the mate wants quick answers. Since the Phlegmatic and Choleric are usually married to each other, it is easy to see their area of financial conflict. The Choleric wants support for his or her daring ventures and the Phlegmatic is running scared, pleading, "Can't you wait and think about it a while?" The Phlegmatic abdicates responsibility to the aggressive Choleric and then is hurt when things don't turn out right. "I should have known," the Phlegmatic says. But when the Phlegmatic is victimized while trying to be the nice guy the Choleric tears into him or her and leaves the peace-lover in pieces.

In her book *Money Makeover,* Rosemarie Patterson suggests that we pair ourselves up with a person of opposite nature to review our financial situation and to make plans for the future. As a bankruptcy attorney, she deals with people for whom, financially, it is already too late. She says if people could only see their personalities and their financial weaknesses, they would not continue to make the same mistakes. So if you are a free-spending Sanguine, find a meticulous Melancholy friend who will help you analyze and plan; you Melancholies find a Sanguine who will insert some fun into your budget. If you are a Choleric, find a gentle Phlegmatic and listen to his or her caution; if you are a Phlegmatic, team up with a Choleric who will add a sense of adventure to your life.

These personality types and their typical attitudes and behaviors about money are shown in the chart on page 79. Find yourself and your mate on the chart, then think about how you can use your differences to complement each other's strengths and weaknesses in managing your finances.

Money Matters according to Personalities

The Popular Sanguine
- Feels money buys *fun*
- Goes in debt for pleasure
- Loves to party and possess
- Cheers up the Melancholy
- Needs to curb spending
- Needs to become disciplined

The Powerful Choleric
- Feels money is *power*
- Goes in debt for risk
- Loves to wheel and deal
- Activates the Phlegmatic
- Needs to listen to advice
- Needs to think before investing

The Peaceful Phlegmatic
- Feels money prevents *problems*
- Goes in debt for others
- Loves to be needed
- Restrains the Choleric
- Tones down the Sanguine
- Needs to loosen up

The Perfect Melancholy
- Feels money is to *manage*
- Goes in debt for the best
- Loves to analyze and correct
- Needs to say no
- Needs to get involved
- Needs to accept others as they are

Recovering from Financial Chaos

One of the main reasons I decided to write this book was to help the endless numbers of fine Christian women who seem to know very little or nothing about finances and are ignorant about their husband's business affairs. Some have been left alone by death or divorce with no understanding of finances and no way to support their families. Others have been brainwashed to think that to be submissive they need to be a little bit stupid. They have been told they have no need to know their financial status because that is man's work. They've been to seminars where they've been instructed to give up their checks, credit cards, and common sense to trust the Lord. This might be acceptable if these women could also trust their husbands to do their part, but what of the wives who have played dumb and lost it all?

79

CLAIMING GOD'S BEST FOR YOUR FUTURE

Dear Florence:

I've been teaching a class at church on making sound investments. I know my business but the class has turned into a marriage counseling course. They're all mad at each other and I seem to have lost control. Can you give me some examples of couples you've worked with that will give me some helpful ideas?

Trying in Tulsa

Dear Trying:

I will be glad to give you examples of women who have overcome trying circumstances to restore their families' financial difficulties. In many cases they denied their own skills in money matters and let their family slip into financial chaos because they thought they wouldn't be good, Christian, submissive wives if they stepped in to advise their husbands.

I'll also offer some sound, practical advice on how to get a handle on one's own financial status and how women should protect themselves in case of their husband's death, divorce, or financial ineptitude.

Millie Misses the Mark

Millie, a Melancholy young woman, approached me with this scenario. Since she was the mathematical and analytical one, she had always taken care of all the finances, giving her Sanguine husband, Mark, a certain amount to have fun with each week. They were both happy with their roles until they went to a Christian seminar on money. This particular speaker explained that God would only bless families where the man was firmly in charge and handled all the money. He had charts and graphs to prove God's plan and at no time did he even infer that some men have no feel for finances. The speaker also didn't take inborn personality patterns into consideration but assumed all men were Choleric (like him) and all women were Phlegmatic (like his wife).

This couple went home under a cloud of guilt, thinking what they had believed was all right was actually all wrong. Reluctantly, Millie gave Mark total control of the bills and the checkbook. She was not supposed to check up on him because that would show a lack of faith. When she came to me six months down the line, the mortgage was overdue, the lights had been turned off, and the phone disconnected. Mark had bought exercise equipment on an installment plan and, typical of the Sanguine male, had run up huge bills taking people out for dinner. She was furious, and he was a bit ashamed of how poorly he'd done.

"Do you think the speaker was right?" Millie asked me.

I reviewed her own story back to her and said, "If someone came to you with this problem, what advice would you give?"

Millie answered, "I'd tell her to take back the responsibility for the bills and the checkbook." And she did.

"I Should Have Stepped in Sooner"

From the time Caitlin and Alex became believing Christians they sincerely desired to serve the Lord and be positive witnesses in their community. They went to church every time the door was opened, attended and taught Bible studies, and ran eagerly to every seminar that passed through town. A confused Caitlin wrote to me:

> Alex and I recently heard you teach on the Personalities and we could see I am Melancholy-Choleric and he is Sanguine-Phlegmatic. Everyone loves Alex, but he didn't do well with our money.
>
> We couldn't find any Scriptures telling us who was to handle the checkbook, or how. I guess there were no banks set up in Bible times and no payment books or credit cards either. We argued over this subject until Alex heard two radio talks that told him the man was the head of the house and should handle the money. Because I had a great desire to be a good, submissive Christian wife, I didn't feel I had the right to challenge my husband's decision to handle the finances, but I hated the bill collectors' calls, and when I mentioned them to my Sanguine husband he'd reply, "No problem. It's my responsibility; don't worry. I'll handle it." Bounced checks didn't bother him, and he couldn't understand why the banks got so upset.
>
> When the first bank closed our account, I was mortified with embarrassment, but Alex happily moved to another bank. He learned

it was even more fun to have more than one account. By writing deposit checks back and forth to each bank he could actually keep things from bouncing longer. At the time neither of us knew this game was called *kiting*. When Alex did write checks, he failed to record them and he never was certain if there was money to cover them. He just wanted to get this no-fun, nonprofitable task over with in one fell swoop. If I objected or made suggestions, he would remind me to be submissive as the radio speakers had taught. Our efforts to follow God's direction, as those speakers presented it, have been disastrous in every way, and, in my opinion, a terrible witness.

Caitlin wrote ten pages of financial crises they had gone through trying to follow what they thought was God's will. Finally, when no bank would give Alex an account, he had to allow Caitlin to take over the finances. By then Caitlin had no respect for Alex's financial abilities and didn't care what any male speaker had to say about finances. As Caitlin got involved in the money problems, she found unpaid taxes, huge interest payments, and general mismanagement.

Soon Caitlin and Alex were studying books on money matters and also reading my *Personality Plus* and Tim LaHaye's *Understanding the Male Temperament*. "Why don't those speakers on male headship know anything about the personalities?" Caitlin asked. "Alex is a great guy, but after reading this material, we realized that he should never have tried to run our finances and I should have used my brain and stepped in sooner."

In addition to taking over their household money, Caitlin encouraged Alex to hire a Melancholy manager for their business who would not write checks on empty accounts. Alex is much happier now that he is freed from responsibilities he hated. He spends his time selling new accounts and has increased the business more than enough to cover the salary of the manager.

Caitlin and Alex are not totally out of the red yet and they still owe the IRS, but they are heading in the right direction. They are current on regular bills, and all their personal charge cards are at a zero balance. Caitlin concludes, "We've updated our wills, prearranged our funerals, and established trusts. Honest, open, noncondemning communication has been the key. I am at peace with my relationship with God, my husband, and our creditors. I know that the Lord will not send more than I can handle. I'm not playing the submissive ostrich anymore. I am outspoken and firm when needed. But I will stand by my man, 'for better or for worse, for richer or for poorer, in sickness and in health, til death do us part.'"

Starting Over Again

Just as Melancholy Millie struggled with the happy-go-lucky Mark, Marcia tried in her gentle, Phlegmatic way to rein in her Powerful Choleric husband, Bill, who was always ready to take on a new challenge. Marcia had been initially attracted to Bill because he was so exciting to be with. There was never a dull moment. Bill made a lot of money and didn't need any advice from Marcia—or anyone else for that matter. As a dedicated Christian, Bill shared everything he owned with Marcia. He put Marcia's name on property, credit cards, loans, and checkbooks, and he frequently had her sign documents, but he refused to explain anything to her, saying, "this is man's work." Marcia told me, "Out of my desire to be a good, submissive Christian wife and obey him in all things, I held back a lot of the time from saying what I really felt."

Bill started out by selling life insurance, and at twenty-three he was the youngest man in the company ever to sell a million dollars' worth in a year, a feat he repeated five times. Then he started opening new businesses on the side and soon had five different businesses going. But he had no time for the details of running them.

Marcia explained, "My husband is optimistic to a fault. He never sees obstacles or problems, only challenges. I describe him as a guy who leaps and then looks for a place to land. Usually he lands on his feet but not always. He's a fast mover and tries to cover all the bases himself. He never hesitates to take a chance. In our twenty-three years of marriage he has made a lot of money, spent a lot of money, and wasted a lot of money."

Bill had exceptional ability, but when he spread himself too thin, he couldn't keep his hands on everything. His new businesses demanded constant cash infusions to keep them afloat, and soon **83**

Bill was having to borrow money. Marcia didn't realize there were serious problems and as the dutiful wife she signed on the loans without question. Soon the whole empire was collapsing around him. As creditors came calling, Marcia was unhappily surprised that her signature stood for responsibility. For the first time in their marriage she had to pay attention to their finances. Bill was forced to talk to her about money and admit that he had made mistakes in his desire to keep his life exciting.

At Marcia's suggestion, Bill agreed to hire some capable, detail-oriented people to help him in his businesses. From that point on, Marcia and Bill discussed his ideas and Marcia helped him put his ambitions into perspective. She signed nothing she didn't understand, and she became his partner in every sense. Marcia is a submissive Christian wife, but she isn't stupid.

"You're a Crook!"

"I'm desperate." The call came to our office early one morning. Joe needed immediate help. "My wife, Janice, threw me out last night and she won't let me back in until I get some counseling." When Joe arrived he seemed like a nice enough person, though slightly disheveled from sleeping in his car all night.

"What is your problem?" we asked.

"I can't understand it. I hadn't done anything wrong and she screamed at me and told me to get out."

"Does she do this often?"

"No, she's usually rational and sane."

"But you can't think of anything that triggered this?"

"Well, it could have been about the money."

The story that followed was what Sanguine/Phlegmatic Joe saw as "no big deal." Janice's father had died recently and Janice had received an insurance payment of fifty thousand dollars. She put it into a joint account in the bank and left it for a rainy day. Janice and Joe had never had any extra money, and Janice, who was a Melancholy, finally felt comfortable to know they had a cushion to fall back on.

One day Janice got a call from the bank notifying her that she and Joe were fifteen thousand dollars behind on their house payments and the bank was going to foreclose. Janice was stunned; she couldn't believe this had happened. Joe was responsible for paying the bills, but since he was out of town at the time, Janice told the bank to take it out of the fifty thousand dollars until she could find out what the problem was. They checked and came back to say, "There is no more money in that account."

Janice was incredulous. Where had the money gone?

When Joe came home, Janice was hysterical. She asked if he knew what had happened and he told her the same thing he told us: "I took out a little when I needed it, but I had no idea it was all gone."

"You're a crook!" she shouted.

Joe always had a look of innocence about him. As a Sanguine who loves to spend money and a Phlegmatic who doesn't bother to keep accounts, Joe had somehow dissipated fifty thousand dollars and run the mortgage into serious arrears. He didn't think he'd done anything that wrong and couldn't imagine why his wife would throw him out.

When Janice came in to see us, she was beside herself. "Did you find out from him what he did with the money?" she begged. We didn't have an answer.

Joe was the bad guy here, but both spouses needed to make changes. Joe didn't like the word *crook* applied to him. He was just *borrowing* the money, he said, and he could legally sign on the account so he wasn't actually outside of the law. When asked how he planned to pay back the "borrowed" money, he had no answer. He hadn't saved even fifty dollars in his life! When we pointed out that this was stealing, he winced. "I've always been very honest," he insisted.

Here was an upstanding Christian man on his church's board of deacons who did not see that taking fifty thousand dollars of his wife's money without asking or mentioning it was dishonest! Nor did he see that while happily spending it all on things that were not additions to the household he had been totally selfish. When we ultimately found out he had gambled with much of it, expecting to pay it back with his winnings, he didn't see that gambling was really a problem. "Not as long as you don't do it a lot," he said. Not paying the mortgage when it was his responsibility **85** didn't strike him as too terrible, either, as the house hadn't been foreclosed on yet.

All of these things added up to a selfish, irresponsible, gambling, spiritual thief who couldn't figure out why his wife was upset with him. Janice was the innocent victim, but what could she have done differently?

First, the fifty thousand dollars should have been placed in an account that was not easily accessible, and Joe and Janice should have discussed what it was to be used for and agreed that neither should touch it for anything else. Second, the insurance money should have been put in an account where two signatures are needed to withdraw money.

But when Janice talked with her pastor about a separate account, he told her that idea was not Christian. He said she needed to be submissive and show her husband she trusted him. She ultimately received more money through her father's estate, and the pastor suggested she put it in the same joint account and pray that her husband wouldn't do the same thing again. Janice asked us if that sounded right to us. You can guess what we told her.

The Other Side—Father Knew Best

Dear Florence:

I've read your stories of financial mismanagement and the men usually seem to be at fault. They spend without counting the cost and don't keep their wives informed on what the limits are. I realize you write these for women, but I've known a few men who get into trouble because their wives have unrealistic expectations and keep pushing to get bigger and better things. We men try to please our wives, but some want too much. Can you share a story that lets women know to not push so much?

Realistic in Reno

Dear Realistic:

You are right. Many of us women are still trying to keep up with the Joneses and some expect a young husband to provide like Daddy

did. For example, Kathleen grew up in a home where her military father had been in charge of all family decisions and especially financial ones. He had been fair with her and her mother, who wrote checks whenever she wished to purchase anything and never had to worry about the balance. Her father's theory was to keep plenty of money in the account and let Mother enjoy life. He was generous and she didn't abuse the privilege. Neither parent ever explained money matters to Kathleen, and she accepted her parents' pattern as the norm. Since they were all Christians, she assumed that if she married a Christian she would have a similar situation.

She met Don at a Christian college and knew he was the right man for her. She never questioned his finances, nor did she express what she expected from him as a husband. Kathleen had no idea that he had some previous debts, so when he selected an engagement ring she persuaded him to buy a more expensive one with a bigger diamond. When he wanted to use some hand-me-down furniture, Kathleen chose a new couch and matching love seat. Don, not wishing to appear cheap or dampen his bride's enthusiasm, let her charge her purchases.

The happiness over her new couch faded when Kathleen found notices of bounced checks and statements with big interest charges in the mail. Don resented her asking about these problems and thought to himself, *If she hadn't wanted the ring and the couch we wouldn't be in this mess.* He thought the money problems were her fault since she had desired too much. He did not add in the burdens and bills he brought to the marriage. Kathleen was resentful that he didn't find money somewhere out of the blue to keep her happy as her father had always done for her mother.

It's easy for us to look at these examples and see objectively how these nice, well-intentioned Christian couples got themselves into financial difficulty that led to marriage problems, but when these spouses were in the throes of quiet anger, neither one could see clearly. Each one buried the resentments he or she felt. Some couples push these hurt feelings down and don't deal with them until the day one of them irritates the other beyond his or her ability to handle it. *Bam!* One explodes and hysterically reviews a litany of **87** mistakes, sending the other into a torrent of angry language that evokes an equally emotional response from the first. Then the cycle continues until doors slam and the combatants withdraw. This scene, however, doesn't put money in the bank!

Fortunately, in Kathleen and Don's case, the spouses were mature enough to pause and assess their problems. Kathleen took over writing the checks and paying the bills. By doing this she got a realistic view of how much money came in compared to what was going out. No more hoping Daddy would just keep filling the well. Kathleen began to look at life as it is. By handling the money Kathleen has more security and she is no longer angry at Don. He is much happier, too, because he is not being compared with Daddy and he doesn't have to buy things he can't afford to make his wife content. Their finances are now a team effort and Don feels the pressure is off.

Kathleen says, "Many Christians buy foolishly on the faith that God will provide. God will bless us much more when He sees we are using common sense."

Role Resentments

Dear Florence:

Well, we did what you told us and we are still miserable! My Phlegmatic husband and I attended your seminar and decided that as the Choleric I should continue to handle our finances. While we both run our own separate businesses, he has not done well with money in the past because he tends to procrastinate the bill paying and the checkbook balancing until there are problems. I agreed to do all his business bookkeeping, as well as my own business and the family accounts. He is not as educated or experienced as I am, so we agreed I should do it.

Now that I have been handling everything for a while, we have both become resentful. You see, while he didn't like the details and responsibility of handling the money, he sure liked having it, spending it, and making decisions about where it was going. Now he feels like I have too much control and he is left out. While I feel "safer" handling the money myself, I realize I am angry because he has gotten out of more work, as usual, by putting the extra load on me. He doesn't work a full forty hours each week anyway and watches afternoon TV talk shows until I come home. Then he asks me, "What's for dinner?" Why should I work full-time, cook, clean, and do all the bookkeeping just because I'm Choleric and he's Phlegmatic? We tried to do what you suggested in your seminar; what went wrong?

Resentful in Riverside

Dear Resentful:

Couples who decide to assign the money management in their family based on the Personalities must also watch out for other potential problems. Resentment will occur when a Choleric or Melancholy takes over the finances from their otherwise gifted Sanguine or Phlegmatic mate unless they deal with their financial ABCs: *authority, balance,* and *communication.*

The mate managing the money will seem to have more control than his or her spouse and must be careful to share the position of *authority* with the other. This means establishing how decisions will be made about major purchases or how financial decisions will be made. Why don't you sit down with your husband and ask him exactly what type of financial decisions he wants to be involved in, making sure you both honestly discuss your fears and concerns. This is a good opportunity for a wife to be submissive in a healthy way, by acknowledging and affirming her husband's needs and rights to be included even in an area she handles.

Balance is important in the division of all family responsibilities, not just handling the finances. If you are better at handling the money than your Phlegmatic husband, can you think of other areas for which you are responsible that he might help you with? Can he cook dinner? Pick up the kids from school for you? Maybe it's time for him to look for a full-time job. While I can't tell you what's right for you in these areas, it's important that you discuss and decide and then pray together about what you can both accept.

Communication means sitting down once a month after you have balanced the budget and sharing the results of the income and

89

expenses with the spouse who hasn't handled the money. This can be done sitting down over coffee on a weekend or as simply as printing out a balance sheet and leaving it on your husband's dresser for him to review. The important thing is that once the decision has been made about who will handle the finances, you must both talk about it as needed or agreed.

Ability to handle money in marriage should be shared. Each spouse should listen to the other's opinion, and each will have his or her own responsibility to keep the other informed.

Eliminating Financial Stress

Dear Florence:

My husband and I divide the responsibility of paying bills and we do pretty well, but I'm never sure he's paid his part and he checks up on me all the time, making me defensive. Do you have some way we could be sure everything is paid on time without double-checking each other? I don't want him looking over my shoulder.

Defensive in Dallas

Dear Defensive:

It sounds as if you two are on the verge of personal problems you don't need to have. I'd like to suggest you do what Fred and I have done, which is to make a simple chart that you can each check without having to ask each other any questions.

No matter who is writing the checks and keeping the finances in order, there needs to be a simple chart that shows what has or has not been paid each month. For years I asked for this and Fred said it was too much work. "Just trust me," he said. I did trust him, but I wanted one place where I could look to see what had been paid. When I had learned that certain bills had added interest charges if paid one day late, I didn't want to be paying one cent extra. Even though nothing was hidden and I could have gone through the checkbooks, I didn't have time to do that. I wanted the information to be on one piece of paper in a simple chart.

Your bills may be very different from mine, but there are certain expenses we all have. The sample chart on page 92 will give you some guidelines. We've divided the types of bills, noted when they are due, and left space where the date they were paid can be written in.

As you can see, the left-hand column lists the bills. In the "Due" column we indicate whether the bill is due on the first or twentieth of the month, twice a year, quarterly or yearly, etc. If a bill is due less often than once a month, we put a little X in the box under the month when it should be paid to serve as a reminder. The person who pays the bill jots down what date he or she paid it so the other person can double-check. Assuming you both do your part, this method will simplify bill-paying and eliminate the question, "Did you pay the rent?"

There are many bookkeeping procedures far more complicated than this and you may be using one, but add this simple record; it will help eliminate stress over money matters and rebuild your trust for each other.

Learning the Laws

Dear Florence:

Please warn the women you teach to find out if they live in a "community property state" or not. I never thought of such a thing, and when my husband divorced me, I found out I was responsible for an expensive painting my husband had bought without a clear title (it was actually stolen property). To stay out of court, I ended up paying more than half of the value to the original owner.

My best friend, upon questioning why her paycheck was smaller than usual, discovered her wages had been garnished by the IRS to pay for her portion of her ex-husband's back taxes. Let women know they must beware of the law, even if they never expect any trouble.

Innocent in Illinois

Dear Innocent:

We women are often too naive. We don't think deviously and we don't think our husbands do either. But ignorance of the law is no excuse.

BILL PAYMENT SCHEDULE

	Due	Jan	Feb	Mar	Apr	May	June	July	Aug	Sept	Oct	Nov	Dec
HOUSE													
Mortgage													
Homeowners Fees													
Yardwork													
Gas													
Electric													
Trash													
Water													
Cable TV													
Phone													
TAXES													
IRS													
State													
CREDIT CARDS													
MasterCard													
Visa													
Department Store													
Other													
INSURANCE													
Life													
Health													
Homeowners													
Car 1													
Car 2													
CARS													
Car 1 Payment													
Car 2 Payment													
Car 1 Tag Renewal													
Car 2 Tag Renewal													

Because each state's financial laws are different, it is important to know what they are. Do you know if your state is "common law" or "community property"? In simple terms common law means the owner of property is the person whose name is on the title. That person can sell, mortgage, or borrow on it without his or her mate's knowledge. Neither partner has a right to the other's wages or belongings.

In contrast, in community property states, including Arizona, California, Idaho, Louisiana, New Mexico, Oregon, Texas, Washington, and Wisconsin, each partner owns half of what was acquired in that marriage and he or she needs the other's signature to sell. You are both responsible for debts, no matter who signed; if he has charged up a storm and then leaves you, you are responsible for half and may be sued for the rest.

No matter which kind of state you live in, a devious husband can find a way to do you in if he sets his heart on it and gets to work on his plan before you know about it. I talk to so many women who say, "My husband is so kind that he'd never do any of those bad things." And I've observed some of the finest Christian men, under the passion of a new love, who lie, cheat, and steal to get all they can. Since their surprised wife is not prepared, feels helpless, and is in a state of shock, the plotting husband and his usually overbearing lawyer can have her begging for any little scrap from the table.

I know one lawyer's wife who didn't even have a table to get scraps from. During dinner one evening, when she was still in shock from the divorce surprise, Joan's husband walked in with some moving men and removed the dining room furniture. The children were left crying on the floor with their plates in their laps. "At least he didn't take the plates out of their hands," Joan said, trying to gain some sense of humor over it all.

Another lawyer sold off property by forging his wife's name and putting the money in his girlfriend's account. By the time the divorce papers came, he was officially destitute and the wife, Peggy, was so confused she couldn't swear she'd not signed the deeds. Under oath she was asked, "Did you ever sign things he brought you without reading them?"

"Oh yes, all the time," she answered, wide-eyed and innocent.

"Then you could have signed these?"

"I guess I could have."

It was all over for Peggy.

While she was on vacation Frannie discovered her husband had been seeing another woman. The following week she came home from her Bible study and found the locks changed on her house. When she located her husband at work, he coldly told her he was divorcing her. His business was about bankrupt, the house was in foreclosure, and she had better find some place to live, he added.

When they got to court, he said he had no income and the house was to be auctioned off the next week. The day before the auction, his brother came forward with the money to redeem it. Frannie got nothing but her clothes; her ex-husband now lives in the house with his new wife and her children.

All of these men are Christians who amazingly have all stayed in the church as leaders. We women must be aware of what's going on with our family finances before it's too late. Not one of these women expected to be divorced. All of them were intelligent Christians, living in lovely homes and what they thought were solid marriages; yet the surprise came to each one. As I talked with them later they had to admit they knew nothing about their husbands' money; they had signed whatever he had handed them and always hoped for the best. It's too late for Joan, Peggy, and Frannie, but how about the rest of us?

"Today no woman should be ignorant of her husband's finances or her own. If a wife doesn't share financial decisions regardless of who earns the money, her husband will act as the powerful daddy. By having to ask, you give up control and then money is used as a reward. Do what your husband would like and he will get you the car you want."[1] So writes Shelby White in *What Every Woman Should Know about Her Husband's Money*, her best-selling book designed to wake women up about the status of their family finances.

According to Kerry Hannon, personal finance reporter for *USA Today*, many women will be on their own one day and will have to manage money solo. The typical widow or divorcee sees her standard of living drop dramatically. Consider the following:

- Ninety percent of women will be solely responsible for their finances at one point in their life.
- Women live an average of seven years longer than men.
- Half of all women married in the past twenty years will eventually divorce.
- Only 15 percent of divorcing women are awarded any form of court-ordered spousal support.
- The typical woman's standard of living dives 45 percent in the first year after divorce while the average man's jumps 15 percent.
- The average age for a woman to be widowed in the United States is fifty-five.

For the first twenty-five years of our marriage, I knew nothing about our family's finances—and I didn't care to know. But as Fred made business mistakes, I realized we had some financial problems. When he informed me we had to sell my dream house, I couldn't believe it. What had happened? The business had steadily lost money, the creditors were pushing, and Fred had to raise cash; that's what happened. I came up with every alternative I could imagine, but the only true solution was to sell the house.

At that point I took a hard look at what I did and didn't know. For example, I didn't know if we had insurance on anything, if we had savings, stocks, bonds, etc., or if we were up to date on our taxes. Since then I have learned I'm not the only intelligent woman who has little information regarding her family's finances. We need to change that and take responsibility for becoming knowledgeable enough about money and business to discuss them intelligently.

Those of us who have better business sense and intuition than our husbands need to get involved in financial decisions that affect our families. But some husbands prefer that we know nothing; if **95** we try to ask questions, they won't give us good answers. Do we accept that, shrug our shoulders, and give up?

Dear Florence:
   Why don't women know more about the family finances? Are the husbands always unwilling to share these matters or are we indifferent or afraid to ask?
                                                                Wondering in Wisconsin

Dear Wondering:
   Not all women want to be bothered, and I have been given many excuses as I've tried to alert women to be knowledgeable. See if any of these sound familiar. Do any apply to you?

____ I trust in the Lord and His provision.
____ I wouldn't dream of questioning my husband.
____ He would never tolerate my interference.
____ He's such an honest man, I don't need to know.
____ He's always handled the money.
____ He makes it; he's got a right to spend it.
____ I don't have time to think about it.
____ I've never been good at figures.
____ As long as he pays the bills I don't care.
____ I wouldn't know what to look for.
____ It's easier to sign things than to read them.
____ He wouldn't tell me the truth anyway.
____ I hate responsibility.
____ If he decides and it's wrong, it's his fault.
____ He says I'm too dumb to understand.
____ I don't think I have a right to know.

   Which reasons ring true for you? Did they point to your unwillingness to learn—time, inability, fear—or were they that your husband doesn't want you to know? If it's your lack of desire, think about the possibility that you might become widowed or divorced or that your husband could become ill and unable to continue bringing in income. If it's because he won't tell you, talk with him about the family finances again, without emotion, and ask him about important financial documents. Let him know that if anything happened to him you wouldn't know what to do. No man ever wants to think he might die, but let him know you need help because you want to feel secure.

Establishing a Credit History

Dear Florence:

My husband and I went to a seminar where we were told to get rid of all our credit cards. We were told Christians shouldn't charge because it's too easy to get into debt. We haven't done this yet, as I feel uneasy about not having credit available. We are not big spenders but the credit cards seem to give me a feeling of security. Am I wrong?

Insecure in Indio

Dear Insecure:

You are not wrong to want credit available when you need it. The principle being taught is probably for those who easily overspend, but in this "no cash" society, as it is being called, credit cards make purchasing and recording our expenditures much easier. As with any desire, we must hold our purchasing within our budget whether we pay cash or charge.

Fred and I each have separate credit cards so I have established a line of credit in my name. Should something happen to Fred, I can rent a house, buy a car, and provide for myself without having to start from zero. These days there are many banks seeking credit card business by giving bonuses for signing. Many are related to airlines and hotels, giving extra points for your travel. We use cards tied to American Airlines and we charge every substantial purchase on these cards. Adding these points to what we get from our frequent flyer miles, we are able to fly to Australia first class once a year for free. In most cases, if you pay your credit card bills within thirty days, there is no interest charge. If you spend without concern, you will of course run up bills too big to pay each month and then be burdened by large interest charges. Sometimes these inter-

97

est and late payment charges can offset your minimum monthly payments so that it may take years to pay off even a small credit card debt.

One friend sat over our coffee table with Fred and me, sobbing, "When my husband and I were both working, we could afford to charge up the credit cards, knowing we could pay them off within a few months at most. But then my husband started to get depressed and he lost many of his customer accounts. I had no idea that his income had dropped in half. Then, after I found out, he left me! I tried to tell the credit card companies that I only had one income now and asked for them to work with me to pay off the debt. You wouldn't believe how cold and uncaring they were! They would only lower the interest rate a little, but the monthly interest is still almost as much as my monthly payment. I couldn't believe it when I found out it will take me fifteen years to pay the card off!"

If you were divorced or widowed, you might have difficulty establishing credit as a single woman. If your credit card is in both your name and your husband's, he could cancel it without your knowledge. If your savings are in both your names, he could withdraw the money unless the card in the bank calls for both signatures. Even then, if the clerk who cashes the check doesn't verify the signature requirements, the money will be gone. To establish credit you need to have a major credit card in your name and a record of having used it. If you make a purchase on credit, use your card and make each payment on time. Don't postpone establishing credit. Tomorrow could be too late.

Insurance, Tax, and Inheritance Issues

Dear Florence:

I hear so much about dumb women who don't know anything about money and who don't even know if their husband has a will. I didn't want to be one of them and I think I've asked all the right questions, but I would appreciate a list of questions for me to consider so I could see if I am missing some answers. I know you

minister to many women who have neglected these areas until it's too late, and perhaps they would like a list also. I don't want to be one of your cases.

Smarter in Savannah

Dear Smarter:

Check out the following items:

____ Does your husband have life insurance and do you know where it is?

____ Do you know how much you would need?

____ Do you know for sure you are the beneficiary?

____ Do you have enough personal life insurance to cover minimal funeral expenses ($5,000)?

____ Do you have health insurance for yourself?

____ Do you have health insurance for your family?

____ Do you know what it covers, how much per day, for how long?

____ Do you carry an insurance card with you in case of an accident?

____ Do you and your husband have disability insurance?

____ Do you know that it only provides about 60 percent of your monthly income and there may be a three-month waiting period?

____ Do you have enough money put aside to cover three months if necessary?

____ Do you have fire and homeowner's insurance?

____ Do you know how much coverage you have and is that enough?

____ Does it cover earthquakes, hurricanes, floods, or other natural disasters?

____ Do you have dental insurance and know what it covers?

____ Do you and your husband each have a signed power of attorney for each other?

____ Do you know what retirement provision you have and who gets what when?

____ Do you have Keoghs or IRAs, and do you know how to use them?

99

____ Do you have your tax returns on file for the seven years the IRS requires?

____ Do you know that if your husband cheats on your joint income tax return and you sign it, you could get in trouble even if you were innocent?

____ Do you know if you have trusts, where they are kept, and who gets what?

____ Do you have a list of all your possessions, estimated worth, and instructions specifying who should inherit each time?

____ Does your husband have an up-to-date will? If he does, do you know where it is and who inherits what? Have you seen and read it?

____ Do you have a will? Or will your children have to fight over the silver set?

These questions are some of the things every woman should know to protect herself from possible disaster. The more times you answer yes, the more you know and the fewer surprises you'll have. If you have answered no to any of these questions, you need to start a learning program *today.*

Unfortunately, we have met widows who found too late that the life insurance went to the first wife and the will was nowhere to be found. We've met divorcées who were done in by their ex-husbands and who were unable to establish any credit.

We don't want to focus on the negative, but we do want to prevent ourselves from being caught off guard.

Dear Florence:

My husband is deeply involved in his family's business. He doesn't have a regular salary, and his father just doles out money when he feels like it. His father owns our house and I have no knowledge of what right we have to anything. He says his father is very fair and I have nothing to worry about, but I'd feel better if I had something in writing. Am I asking too much?

Brooding in Boston

Dear Brooding:

No, you are not asking too much. You are in a frightening situation. If your husband were in an accident tomorrow, you have no assurance your father-in-law would continue to support you. You must get some legal counsel and have protective papers drawn up that will spell out what you do and don't possess. You husband must have a will that provides for you.

Your story reminds me of Gladys, who came to me one afternoon. As we sat and talked at dinner that night, she poured out her story. Her husband's family had a manufacturing business, and when the father died, Gladys's husband, Ray, inherited two-thirds of the business and his brother one-third. Ray was the salesman and his charming personality was the ingredient that doubled the business in five years' time. Gladys was thrilled with the additional income they received and happily spent it on new furniture, jewelry, and cars. She knew nothing about the business or the prospects for the future. Ray felt invincible and didn't like to focus on the negatives. But suddenly Ray dropped dead.

At the funeral his brother mentioned to Gladys that he was in charge now and he hoped Ray had adequate insurance to keep her going. Gladys was in a double state of shock, first with the sudden death and then with her brother-in-law's casual comment. As soon as she was emotionally able, Gladys went to the office to straighten out the finances and find out what her share was. Her in-laws let her know she had no share. The business was the family's and she was no longer a part of it.

"What am I to live on?" she asked.

"That's your problem," they answered.

"But Ray inherited two-thirds of the business," Gladys cried.

"What proof do you have? Do you have any document that says so?"

She didn't. In fact Gladys had no idea what she did or didn't own. In checking she found Ray had minimal insurance and had never increased it when he started making more money. The IRS put a hold on his bank account and Gladys found herself with high mortgage payments, cars bought on credit, and no cash in hand. **101**

When she appealed to her in-laws, they scoffed at her and loaned her a thousand dollars—with interest. None of her friends took pity on her as she had the biggest house of the group; they soon tired of what they called her "poverty pleading."

Gladys ultimately found a lawyer who thought she had a case against her in-laws. It took eighteen months and twenty thousand dollars to finally get a legal subsistence allowance from the business. By that time Gladys had been forced to sell the house and all but one car in order to stay alive.

Whatever you do, get it in writing, make sure you have a separate lawyer from the family, and have the lawyer keep signed copies of everything. You don't want to become a case history.

Marriage Contracts

Dear Florence:

My name is Lisa and I am thirty years old. I have four children ages six, four, two, and six months, and my husband was in a new business that wasn't making any money when my mother died in a car crash. When I was grieving over my mother's death and expecting sympathy, all my husband said was, "We all have to die sometime." He doesn't seem to have any feeling about anything. I have tried to get him to realize how much I miss my mother. She was my comforter. I realize that Tom has never understood me emotionally and I got so upset that I moved out to my girlfriend's house with my children.

When I went to a lawyer to see what my options were, he told me because I'd only been married seven years I could expect no alimony. He told me ten years seems to be the magic number for any leverage, and I didn't have it. I told the lawyer I had helped start my husband's business. Wouldn't that make a difference? Apparently not. He assigned me to do some research looking up papers and information. I had no idea where anything was, but I began a search. I found out that both the cars and all the credit cards were in my husband's name. I checked the joint bank account and found all the money was gone.

Here I was with no degree, no job, no expertise, and in effect no husband. The lawyer didn't give me much hope since my husband had put all the money into his business. I realized I had suddenly become one of the great American homeless living below the poverty line. What do I do now?

Lonely Lisa in Lincoln

Dear Lonely Lisa:

What a mess you're in! Your moving out so quickly after your mother's death was not a wise move, but since you've done it, we have to go on from there. Call your husband and see if he is willing to talk with you about coming back. Your four children do need a father. If he will talk, meet with a lawyer and lay out what changes need to be made for you to start over again. Don't go back until you know he's willing to be open about money and business. You can't make him be sympathetic, but you can ask him to give you the security and information you need. Let me know what happens.

It was a few months before I heard back from Lisa. She had called her husband, who played hard to get but who agreed to meet with a lawyer. When they saw each other they both hugged and began to cry. He showed emotion as she'd always wanted him to do. The lawyer suggested they sign a contract with each other on the changes they were willing to make so she would have a sense of security.

Their contract specifies that her husband would buy her a car in her name, and he did. She now has a separate bank account, and at the end of each year, she and her husband review their finances and divide the assets in half. "I am now with him by choice, not by control," Lisa wrote. "I realize I'd been all messed up by my upbringing about what *submission* means. I had let Tom do whatever he wanted and this had led to both financial and sexual problems. I allowed him to treat me like a piece of property."

Their business has prospered since they got their finances straightened out. "I could leave tomorrow," Lisa writes, "with over $150,000 in assets all my own, but I don't want to leave a man who has given me freedom to be an intelligent wife and an equal partner."

One other agreement they have in the contract was a new thought to me. The bedroom is Lisa's and she chooses to share it with her **103** husband. Before, he demanded sex no matter how Lisa felt; now he courts her and treats her like a lady. Not a bad idea!

Financial Checklist

Women need to be sure that we have access to and understand all of our family's finances. We shouldn't be caught unaware if we are left on our own because of death or divorce. Let's consider the following questions as we set out to be financially informed.

If you needed to, would you know where to find birth certificates for each member of the family? Your marriage certificate? Title to each car? Insurance policies? Mortgages? Stocks and bonds?

If you lost your wallet, do you have a list of all credit cards and their numbers?

Do you have your driver's license number and social security number written down where you can find it outside of your wallet?

Do you know about each bank account, whose name it's in, and who can withdraw from it?

Do you have a savings and checking account in your name that no one else can touch?

Do you have a major credit card and at least one card from a department store in your name?

If you have answered yes to all of these questions, you are an exceptional woman, way above average!

When Submission Allows Abuse

In June 1992 the American Medical Association declared domestic violence against women to be a national epidemic. Abuse in the home is the leading source of injury for women between the ages of fifteen and forty-four. One-third of the women who are brought to emergency rooms are victims of domestic violence, and over four million women each year are severely assaulted by their present or former mate. Because of these increasing statistics, the AMA has issued directives for its members to guide them in looking for and reporting domestic-violence cases.[1]

As we approach the new millennium, the statistics have improved somewhat but the problem is still critical. The *Los Angeles Times* reported that 14 percent of women coming into Los Angeles hospitals are willing to say that they are being abused, but many that are obviously victims cover up and defend the abuser. One in three women in the largest survey ever done on this subject admit they have been abused at some time in their life. The fact that this survey was not restricted to inner-city teaching hospitals shows how widespread the problem is.[2]

On February 7, 1999, *Los Angeles Times* printed a report on a new program to help protect domestic violence victims. The article defined domestic violence as "willful infliction of corporal injury resulting in a traumatic condition perpetrated against a spouse, cohabitant, or person with whom the perpetrator has a child." Because of repeated victimization, there is a need for protection and the state of California now offers a free post office box for mail forwarding and keeping records confidential. This is a big step in the wide-spread abuse problem. As it has been in the past, women and children "continue to live in fear, literally dropping out of sight and starting all over again. They cannot talk to their families or friends. They cannot go to the grocery store and use an ATM card. They're not able to have a phone. They cannot go back to where they worshipped."

Even though electronic database compound this problem, this new program is a step forward. Currently Washington, Massachusetts, New Jersey, Florida, and Nevada have similar programs. This is an honest-to-goodness effort by the government to assume that women who have been victimized will no longer be victimized again.

Are any of these abuses taking place in Christian homes? Or are we better than the rest? Unfortunately, Christians tell me stories of domestic violence each week. And Christian leaders often respond to victimized wives with direction to "just be more submissive and you will win him by your 'sweet and gentle spirit.'" How long is a woman—any woman—to be sweet, gentle, submissive—and beaten up? One pastor told a lady, "You will get your reward in heaven." She was on her way.

The stories in this chapter are based on real women in real situations. They describe the abuse of Christian wives by their Christian husbands. In most cases these wives accepted the abuse, thinking they had no choice if they were to be good, submissive Christian wives. But as I pointed out earlier, being submissive doesn't mean being victimized.

A Pattern of Victimization

Dear Florence:

I am a Sanguine who has not had a happy moment for years. My mother told me I was too loud and always looking for attention so I learned my personality was not acceptable. I married someone who doesn't approve of anything I do and who abuses me both verbally and physically. I would like to tell you the whole story and get your advice. How could I get to see you?

Beaten in Buffalo

I invited this woman to a seminar in her area. When I met Polly she was overweight, depressed, and discouraged. She shared memories of being sexually abused by her grandfather and upon reporting the abuse, her mother saying, "Whatever your grandfather does is all right. We're living in his house and if you don't please him, he'll throw us out on the street and it will be your fault." Not only was Polly living under the rule of conditional love, but she was also being sexually abused and had no recourse. Everything was always her fault. Is it any wonder Polly's adult life was sprinkled with guilt?

Polly told me how she had grown up with a Melancholy martyr mother and a father who was Sanguine with his friends but Phlegmatic at home. The mother waited on them all, sighed often, and made frequent note that she never did anything for herself, only for others. "Your father always knows that if I'm not doing for him, I'm doing for you children." Polly was taught that women are inferior and must accept their lot in life. Being subservient, she believed, is being godly.

Polly is a Sanguine and she knew from the beginning she didn't fit with the rest of the family. Because she didn't like the quiet morbidity she felt at home with her family, she went outside to have fun and tried to be the dutiful child when she was at home. Her mother kept pointing out that Polly was different and if she'd only think of others and give more of herself she would be accepted. "If I could just be better," Polly recalls thinking, "maybe I'd be accepted. If I could just be that gentle, kind, giving person I *should* be, then I'd be OK in everyone's sight and wouldn't have so many problems. And if I do as my grandfather says, he'll let us stay."

Polly tried so hard, but all she got for her efforts was the warning: "You are just an ordinary person. Don't try to inflict yourself on those above you."

Polly was desperate for love, attention, and affirmation and when she found a boyfriend who seemed to like her, she was willing to do whatever he wanted. Polly got pregnant at sixteen and "brought disgrace upon the family." She was forced to get married quickly and leave town so no one would know the truth. When her sister got married in a lavish ceremony a few years later, Polly was told, "You could have had a wedding like this if only you'd been good."

Polly tried to be good, and she knew from her saintly mother that a good wife was submissive and did what pleased her husband. Polly asked herself, "Oh, how many times as a child had I gotten hit with the belt or been grounded because I had a will of my own? When would I learn that if I was what others wanted me to be I would be accepted? When would I learn that I was nothing if I was not what others wanted me to be?"

With this distorted view of what a good Christian wife was, Polly really tried. At first her young husband criticized whatever she tried to do. "I thought if I could just stir the sauce clockwise instead of counterclockwise maybe he wouldn't hit me," she said. "If I could just cook all three vegetables he brought home, maybe he wouldn't yell at me in front of my friends. If I could just learn to clean like my mother. If only . . . if only . . ."

The verbal abuse gradually turned into shoving and hitting, but Polly felt she deserved whatever she got. After all, she wasn't perfect. "With no self-esteem, no self-worth, and no self-love left, I finally gave in and did as I was told," she said.

But her obedience didn't stop the abuse. This was a husband who hadn't wanted to get married in the first place, and he took his anger out on Polly. When he threw her to the floor, sexually victimized her, and tried to choke her, she finally woke up. She knew if she didn't do something to change things she'd be dead within the year either by his hand or her own.

She called her mother, who told her she needed to be more submissive, and her pastor, who said he'd pray for her. Close to hysterics, Polly phoned her friend, who said, "Get out of there immediately and come to my house."

For a year Polly and her two sons lived in one room of her friend's house until she could save enough for a deposit on an apartment. They tried to hide from her husband in fear he would continue to abuse them. By the time we began to work with Polly, she had healed enough to be able to understand her deep feelings of rejection and abuse. Her parents, not understanding her Sanguine personality or her emotional needs, had taught her she was unacceptable as she was. Her mother had dismissed her reports of being abused by her grandfather so as not to upset their living arrangements. This added guilt to the abuse. Polly's marriage was doomed from the beginning because she accepted abuse as what she deserved. When she asked for help, she was told all her problems were her own fault. She didn't believe she had the right to assert herself and take charge of her life.

As Polly saw the connection between her childhood abuse and her spousal abuse and began to see she was a worthy person in God's sight, she was able to see light at the end of the tunnel. Fred taught her to write her prayers each day, seeking healing from the Lord. I helped her see her talent and possibilities. Polly's marriage was not restored, but she has raised two successful sons and now helps other abused women who need to talk to someone who's been there, not someone who says, "It must be your fault. If only . . ."

How many of you women have been made to feel you are to blame for everything that's ever happened to you or your family? You are not the sole cause of your problems. Begin to prayerfully look at your childhood to find the root cause of your adult pain. Don't let your mother, pastor, or friend drape unnecessary guilt around your shoulders. Hebrews 12:1–2 tells us to "lay aside every weight, and the sin which doth so easily beset us" so that we can "run with patience . . . the race, looking unto Jesus the author and finisher of our faith." Some of us women have been so burdened and so blamed that we are not even in the race. We don't feel worthy to enter a contest we know we will lose.

Not until Polly examined her childhood pain and found the core problem of both verbal and sexual abuse was she able to lay aside her weights and enter the race. As an added bonus Polly has **109** lost some of the extra weight she put on as a wall of protection around her, and her Sanguine personality is bursting forth as she shares her healing process for the glory of God the Father.

"You Are an Abused Woman"

Dear Florence:

I am an abused wife who has been repeatedly victimized by my "fine" Christian husband. My pastor doesn't believe my story because he says my husband prays so well at prayer meeting. I went to a counselor who asked me what I had done to provoke my husband's anger. He hits me just as much when I'm docile as when I fight back. Am I the only women being beaten by a praying husband?

Caroline Christian

Dear Caroline:

No, you are not the only woman being abused by a Christian husband. There is no quick fix for your situation, but if you both want to hold your marriage together the Lord can do wonders for you.

Caroline's story is similar to Polly's but it has a better ending. She and Peter were both expressive Christians when they met. They had similar interests and hobbies and prayed together on each date. Caroline noticed Peter's occasional burst of anger, but she could always rationalize that some circumstance had caused it. Soon after their wedding, Peter began to put Caroline down, discourage any activities she wanted to attend, and show jealousy toward her family. She tried to tell herself this was his way of expressing love but his angry tirades became more frequent and there no longer seemed to be any cause for them. Caroline believed as a Christian she had to deal with the hurts she felt as her cross to bear. She also believed she had to accept Peter the way he was.

"For seven years," Caroline wrote, "we lived a roller-coaster marriage, either high on the mountaintop or way down in the valley. Peter's emotions were either ecstatic or combinations of despair mixed with frustration, anger, and depression. Throughout these years I was receiving mixed messages. Peter would fly into fits of rage and violently abuse me; then, after he'd calmed down, he would profess love to me and buy me gifts and flowers with love notes tucked inside. He spent an enormous amount of money we didn't have in trying to make up for the hurts he caused."

Finally Caroline listened to her sister, who had observed Peter's fits of rage and told her, "You are an abused woman. You must do something before you are killed!" Caroline hadn't thought of herself as abused, but as her sister reviewed the symptoms, she listened and agreed. Caroline and her sister managed to convince Peter to go to a psychiatrist, who tried to teach him how to control his anger but never sought the source of his volatile emotions.

Caroline wrote, "I knew I couldn't take the abuse any longer. I had exhausted all of my personal resources trying to get along and be gentle and kind, but nothing I ever did calmed him down." At the insistence of her family, Caroline moved her belongings to another town. When Peter came home to an empty house, he was horrified. *She must mean business,* he thought.

As Peter saw that Caroline was upset enough to leave, he began to get serious about his anger problem. He knew it was God's will for them to stay married, and he began to pray, study God's Word, and seek Christian counseling.

By the time Caroline and Peter came to our Promise of Healing Workshop they were close to desperate. Peter was ready to look at the sexual abuse in his childhood. This took the cover off his anger and let him vent to the Lord the source of his anger, the horror he had lived through. Peter's abusive treatment of Caroline had nothing to do with who she was or how she behaved. It was Peter's unconscious response to what had been done to him as a child. As the pressure receded in Peter's life, Caroline was free to deal with the childhood abuse in her own past.

In contrast to Polly, who fled for her life and, instead of getting help in restoring her marriage, received only condemnation for leaving, Caroline and Peter worked together to find the heart of their abusive marriage and then put it back together again. Healing is a process, not an event, and Caroline and Peter now are on the road to recovery. Caroline wrote, "We learned that any abuse we received as children has an emotional impact on us as adults. Peter didn't abuse me because he was a bad person, but because he was so angry inside. Thank you for helping us take the cover off our pain and begin the healing process."

Grieving for What Might Have Been

Dear Florence:

I think I've made so many mistakes in allowing myself and my children to be hurt that we'll never recover. Is there anything I can do?
Despairing in Dublin

Dear Despairing:

It may seem you'll never overcome your past mistakes. You certainly can't change your past, but you can try to change your future. Listen to Vera's story and learn from her example.

I first met Vera when she came to CLASS to learn how to be a Christian speaker. She had already been teaching Bible studies and was involved in a Christian ministry. When she had an opportunity to speak in the small group session at CLASS, Vera told her story.

When Vera was nine years old, she was molested on a Saturday afternoon at the movies by the man sitting next to her. He told her she was a good girl and gave her two dollars. She remembers how fast she ran to spend the money to get it out of her hands. Even at nine she knew this was "dirty money." She told her father what had happened and he laughed at her. "You should be glad a man looked at you," he chided. "You're so homely. You'll never find another man who'll think you're worth two dollars."

From then on Vera believed she'd never find a man who'd think she was worth anything. Her father continued to verbally abuse her and when at eighteen she found a boyfriend who said he loved her, she married him.

Her mother begged her not to marry the boyfriend. She pointed out how rough he was with her and how they fought and argued all the time. This young man was a replica of Vera's father, and the mother could no doubt see the handwriting on the wall. But the couple went ahead with their wedding plans.

A year later Vera had a son; suddenly there was something beautiful in her life. But her husband was jealous of her attention to the son and verbally abused her just as her father had done. Then the abuse became physical; one night he held Vera down on the bed with a butcher knife at her throat for over two hours, teaching her submission. Vera was afraid she'd be killed at any moment. When she finally got loose, she began to plan her escape. Her husband told her she'd never get away from him because if he couldn't have her, he'd make sure no one else would either. One night when he sensed she might escape from the prison he had made for her, he came up behind her and strangled her. When she passed out and fell to the floor, he left, thinking he had killed her. She awoke, grabbed the baby, and ran to a neighbor's house to call the police. They picked up her husband and put him in jail for thirty days.

When he got out, he didn't come near her or their son. Nor did he send money. Vera had nowhere to turn. She couldn't admit to her mother that she had been right about her husband, so when he finally called and said he'd changed, Vera let him back in. She needed money and she wanted to save face.

For a while he was better, but soon he started abusing her again. He told the little boy what a rotten mother he had and he gave the child anything he wanted. Vera didn't know where to go for help; in desperation she ran away and left her son behind. In the divorce proceedings that followed, Vera had poor legal counsel and lost custody of her son to her husband, believing she'd be able to visit him and maintain contact, but once the divorce papers were signed it was all over. Each time she'd try to see her son the new wife would scream at her and the ex-husband would curse at her. Miserably, she'd stand near the boy's school and watch him go in with the others. The few times he saw her, he would look the other way. She wrote his school and asked for a copy of his report card and a school picture, which they sent. Later she received a letter from the school saying since she was not the legal guardian she would not be allowed to have his records again or come onto the school grounds.

Vera's son is now in his thirties, and Vera has not talked to him since the day she left. She occasionally tries to contact him, but she receives no reply. Nor has she received any answers to the letters she sent to him. Vera assumes he has been so brainwashed against her, the mother who "rejected" him, that she may never see him again. Vera never had another child and she grieves for what might have been. "When you are in the middle of these problems," Vera says, "you can't see the whole picture and you think you have no choice."

Vera's second husband has treated her well and they are on the staff of an international Christian organization. She has come to CLASS to prepare herself to speak to young women in the hope that she will be used to spare others.

When I was preparing to write this, I asked Vera if I could share her story.

"The reason I haven't told my story before," Vera said, "is that I didn't think anyone would believe me. But the Lord urged me to use it to help women take control of their lives. If one woman can be spared the lifelong heartache I have suffered, it will be worth risking the embarrassment."

Here's some of the advice Vera now offers others contemplating marriage:

1. **Don't marry as an escape.** There's got to be another way. If your living situation is abusive, go to a relative you trust or to the authorities, who are much more aware of these problems today than they were twenty years ago. Do whatever you have to do to be safe, but don't marry someone to escape problems at home and then start a family that may well be as dysfunctional as the one you left. Ask your parents and friends how they perceive the potential of this marriage and listen to what they say.

2. **Look at your father's weaknesses.** Ask yourself if there are any similarities between your father's and your fiancé's weaknesses. Are the things you're trying to flee already apparent in even a small way in this new person? It's tragically ironic but true: We tend to marry the same kind of behavior we're

trying to escape. In case after case I see the same kind of abuse going from generation to generation.

3. **Don't marry a non-believer.** So often young girls in the flush of what appears to be love think it doesn't matter that much if he's a Christian. Many think, *He'll become a believer living with me!* Not so. Seldom will a young man who won't commit his life to Christ before marriage suddenly convert on his honeymoon. God wouldn't have told us not to be unequally yoked for no good reason. The devil can use an atheistic husband to ruin the wife and spread strife in the family.

Calling the Cops on a Cop

Dear Florence:

For several months now my husband has been accusing me of cheating on him. I try not to get defensive, but it's hard when he gets so upset and physically threatens me. He says he can't trust me and that my actions make him unable to control his temper. What should I do?

Scared in Sacramento

Dear Scared:

Your actions aren't the problem; your husband's temper is. Don't let him manipulate you into accepting his violence. A friend of mine confronted a similar situation in her marriage.

Patsy's husband was a policeman trained to look at circumstances, people, and their actions and quickly come up with an accurate assessment and a course of action.

Patsy had always been the sweet, dutiful wife. It was not until she had been married to Pete more than twenty years that she went back to work part-time in an office. At first there was no problem with her working, but as time went on and she began to express to Pete how good it felt to be appreciated for her hard work and how much she enjoyed what she was doing, she sensed that this made Pete feel threatened.

One night Pete announced to Patsy she was going to quit her job the following month and there would be no discussion about   **115** what she wanted. When he couldn't get his point across, Pete finally accused Patsy of being attracted to her boss.

He knew in his heart that she had always been a faithful wife, but to get control of her he accused her of planning to run off with her boss. Throughout the next year, whenever Patsy didn't jump to his every desire, Pete would bring up the supposed affair, threaten her again, and leave with a dramatic slam of the door. Sometimes he stayed away a few hours, sometimes several days. Patsy, the perpetually submissive wife, was dumbfounded that after all these years of apparent harmony, Pete was playing havoc with her emotions.

She suggested counseling, but Pete refused to even consider it. "There's nothing wrong with me. If you'd quit your job and stay home, we'd have no problems," he fumed.

Pete became paranoid when none of his offers or threats seemed to work. One night he came storming in holding a cassette tape in his hand. "I have the proof!" he shouted. "I have a tape of you and your boss. I have proof you're having an affair."

If Patsy had been involved, she might have been done in by this supposed proof, but since she was innocent she was able to be strong and say, "That's a lie. There is no affair and no proof."

Pete was furious that his trick hadn't worked and he backed Patsy up against the kitchen sink and berated her in a barrage of verbal abuse. Towering over her nose to nose, he threatened to hit her. Patsy had little hope of pushing away a man who could subdue violent criminals, but she tried. As she shoved him, he hit her. They were both stunned. How could their good marriage have turned to this? What should the sweet submissive wife do at this point? Just what Patsy did.

She ran to the phone and called 911.

The whole time she was on the phone with the dispatcher, Pete was telling her how stupid she was for calling. This was the worst thing she could've done, he said. When the officers arrived, they asked Pete to leave and go to the station to be interviewed. They interviewed Patsy at home, and she asked that Pete not be allowed to come home.

Pete was a man out of control. He didn't know how to deal with a situation when control was taken away from him. The only way he knew how to handle the problem was with anger, threats, and finally violence. Patsy did the right thing; she stopped the violence at the start. Then she set down some conditions for their relationship in order for them to be reconciled: Pete would go to counseling with her until the *counselor* said he could quit coming, and there were to be no threats, no physical abuse, no accusations of affairs with her boss. Finally, decisions about her job wouldn't be made by Pete, but by Patsy; he would support her career as she had supported his.

Patsy was courageous to call 911. She realized it might signal the end of a twenty-five year marriage, but she also realized she didn't want to continue in a lifestyle she had seen so many other women put up with year after year. Sometimes love must be tough and set parameters in order to stay on solid ground. Love means allowing our mates to be who they are, accepting them, and wanting them to be fulfilled and happy. *We* cannot be their happiness or their all-in-all.

Patsy's friend shared with her the image that spouses are two people choosing to ride bicycles in the same direction—not on a tandem bike where one leads and the other follows unquestioningly, but on two different bicycles, choosing to go in the same direction. Sometimes one is ahead, sometimes another, and sometimes they ride along at the same pace, but they're always choosing to travel in the same direction.

You have some difficult choices to make. If your husband lays a hand on you, you must take action. Do as Patsy did—set some parameters and take some steps that will get you both back on your bikes, moving in concert, and heading by choice in the same direction!

The Big Why

Why did Polly stay so long in an abusive marriage? Why did Caroline put up with Peter's abusive anger? Why did Vera not fight for her rights? Why did these women seem to attract men who demeaned them and physically abused them? Was it something they were doing? Did they have offensive personalities? Were they not perfect enough?

No! This had nothing to do with it. All of these women had been abused as children by their parents, so even as adults they felt they deserved nothing better. Why didn't they call 911 as Patsy did? Because they didn't know they had a right to stand up for themselves. They believed the lies told to them by parents, by friends, by colleagues: "You must have done something to deserve it" or "All of us have our crosses to bear" or "Why do *you* make me do this?" or "If you'd only behave, it wouldn't happen" or "You made your bed; now lie in it."

But Patsy knew she didn't deserve to be slapped. She knew she had the right to stand up for herself—to take control of a forboding situation. She didn't wait to see if Pete would hit her again or if the rage would pass. Pete learned right then that this behavior would not be accepted. He would certainly think twice about ever laying a hand on Patsy again!

Are you believing lies fed to you by others? Do you *know* that you have a right to stand up for yourself? If *push* came to *shove,* literally, what would *you* do? No matter what any well-meaning person may have told you, you don't become a non-Christian because you take charge of your life and refuse to be abused.

How to Stop Being a Victim

There are no magic tricks to restore order in an abusive marriage, but here are some positive suggestions that have worked for others.

- **Get out quickly.** Do not pass go. Do not collect two hundred dollars! Take your keys, purse, and your kids and go! If he has abused you before and you think it might happen again, take some things over to a friend's house—a few changes of clothes, extra toiletries (include some cash in this bag for safety's sake), and the children's needs for a few days (clothing, a toy, etc.). If violence does occur, either go to the friend's home or to a motel, your parents, or a shelter.
- **Don't go to another man.** Think about the long-term consequences. If your marriage ends in separation or divorce, you certainly don't want your husband to be able to produce pictures, tapes, or other accusations of your abandoning the mar-

riage because of another man. You also don't want him to convince the court that your affairs during the marriage make you an unfit mother so he gets custody of the children.

- **Don't leave the children there.** You don't want them to be subjected to any of his anger or abuse when he finds you have left. If you do leave them, your husband's attorney will bring up the fact in court that you must have abandoned them and that you must also feel your husband's fathering skills were not lacking or you would not have left them with him.

- **Get medical attention.** If you've been injured by your husband, don't be embarrassed at how you look and don't be ashamed of what's happened—just get help. Be sure you get a copy of the bill for treatment or a copy of the report from the emergency room or doctor's office. You *must* document the abuse in case you need to prove it in court.

- **Don't lie.** When you report the abuse, tell the story just as it happened. Professional people (doctors, police, nurses) see this abuse day after day. Your situation is not unique. Don't cover up for him, and be sure to let them know there have been other instances of violence if that is the case.

- **Make a police report.** If you call 911 this happens anyway, whether or not you want to press charges of spousal abuse. If you call the local police or sheriff directly, make sure they make a report.

- **Get a restraining order.** Go to the courthouse in your county or city (any police department can tell you where to get this) and file a restraining order against your abusive husband. Be sure to file this with the appropriate jurisdiction. If you file in a city and you live in the county, the county sheriff will have no jurisdiction on the restraining order. When you file you must explain why you need it, and you must be able to articulate a fear of violence, harassment, or threats. This restraining order is not a guarantee of your safety, but it will document the fact that you were afraid. The fee for filing varies from place to place, but several I've checked were between fifty and seventy-five dollars. Call the appropriate law enforcement agency if your husband violates the order. The only way the police can help is if they are called. If the man shows up in violation of this order, *call the police.* If your husband is violent or is threatening you, be sure to tell the 911 operator and have him or her stay on the line with you until help arrives.

- **Get a safe-deposit box.** Unfortunately, if there's been abuse in the past there is a great likelihood it will occur again, so you must plan ahead. Go to the bank and rent a safe-deposit box. Here is an idea of some of the things you should have in it:

  1. Extra keys to the house, car, etc.
  2. Extra blank checks from your *own* account
  3. Duplicate credit cards (your *own,* not in *his* name)
  4. Two hundred dollars in cash (more if you can afford it)
  5. Copies of the wills, bank statements, credit card bills, marriage certificates, birth certificates, and the restraining order, if applicable
  6. Photos of past injuries due to violence
  7. Copies of police reports, etc., detailing past violence

- **Take color pictures.** Take pictures of the house in disarray, or broken furniture or windows, and of the children, frightened and hurt. Have someone else take pictures of you including close-up shots of bruises and lacerations. A video tape with the date in the corner of the frame would also be excellent evidence. This may sound ridiculous now, but I've had so many women say later, "I wish I'd had the proof."

- **Remove known weapons.** If there is a gun in the house, temporarily remove it. You could put a small handgun in the safe-deposit box, but a larger one may need to be placed in someone else's custody so your husband will not be able to use it to hurt you, your children, or himself in a moment of rage. Certainly it is hoped that, with counseling, this terrible time in your marriage will pass and you will no longer have to hide guns and worry for your safety. But wouldn't it be horrendous if you decided not to take precautions like these and the worst-case scenario unfolded? The newspaper is full of such sad stories every day!

- **Press charges and stick with them.** If you value your life and your children's lives, proceed with the charges. Don't just assume your violent husband will reform tomorrow.

In her book *Love and the Law,* Gail J. Koff says, "It is our experience that there is a continuing pattern to abuse and unless the couple seeks professional help, the problem is almost sure to recur. The frustrating fact is that most women, if they do seek the help of legal authorities, eventually drop the charges against the men who batter them."[3]

Isn't it time we women realize that we do not deserve to be abused and mistreated? We have the God-ordained right to demand we be treated in a healthy way.

Scripture tells us "Woman is the glory of the man" (1 Cor. 11:7). She is not a doormat, a victim, or a possession.

seven

Sticks and Stones
Can Break My Bones,
and Words Can Also Hurt Me

Dear Florence:

My husband insults me in front of other people, ridicules me before the children, and thinks threats and foul language are funny. I've talked to my friends about this and they say, "Be glad he's not beating you." I'm scared he will someday. I'm not the same upbeat personality I used to be. Is this a form of abuse?

Frightened in Forestville

Dear Frightened:

What a shame that your husband thinks it's funny to insult and demean you. Yes, this is a form of abuse. Remember the old saying, "Sticks and stones will break my bones, but words can never hurt me"? That might work for first graders (probably not though), but it doesn't do much to cheer up women who are being called insulting names and ridiculed by their husbands in front of others.

Many women I meet are not being beaten or burned, yet their beaten-down attitudes, looks, and burned-out existence scream abuse. Not all abuse is physical. The dictionary defines the verb *abuse* as "to attack in words, to put to an improper use, to use so as to injure or damage."

The first part of the definition refers to a verbal attack. Men frequently feel that strong language and swearing are indications of being a real man, but this attitude easily leads to verbal abuse. As with physical violence, abusive words express the victimizer's need to dominate and control. An article entitled "The Wounds of Words" in the October 12, 1992 issue of *Newsweek* explains that verbal abuse can take the form of anger, ridicule, undermining, constant judging, or challenging:

> The verbal abuser has a different style and a different motivation. He uses words and emotions (like anger and coldness) to punish, belittle, and control his partner and he does it compulsively and constantly. He rarely apologizes and shows little empathy.
>
> As a power play, the war on words can be devastatingly effective; many targets of abuse start to believe the put downs they hear.

Since verbal abuse doesn't leave physical scars, it is difficult for the hurting victim to find help. Since you are the victim of verbal abuse and feel helpless, confront your husband. You may need a friend, pastor, or counselor with you for protection and reinforcement when you do this. Let him know you are sure he doesn't mean to hurt you but that you will not be able to continue to live in a verbally abusive situation. State clearly what the abuse is, give examples of the abuse, and describe what you expect from here on. You must set limits no matter what the abuse is and let the abuser know that the next time is the last time.

A decent man will not want to be abusive once he sees what he's been doing, but a sick, angry man may not improve. In fact, if he came from an abusive background, he may go from verbal to physical abuse. You must stop him before it's too late and the words turn into violence. Arrange a meeting with a counselor with whom he can work through the source of his anger and his need to put you down.

Is This Abuse?

Dear Florence:

How do I know if I am being abused? I grew up in a family where drinking, swearing, vulgar language, and an occasional swat across the face were normal. I'm married to a man who's just like my crude father. I didn't see it before we were married because I wanted to get away from home and my husband was available. I feel my parents' home was dysfunctional, but my mother says it was normal. When I complain about my husband, she says, "I lived through it, so you can too." This doesn't cheer me up much. Am I crazy or what?

Crazy in Cincinnati

Dear Crazy:

You are not crazy and you did come from a dysfunctional family according to your description. Unfortunately, you have done what many young girls do, jump from the frying pan into the fire. Your husband, having seen your family, doesn't think he's doing anything wrong. His family was probably the same. If he's a person who wishes to improve his lot in life, he will respond to your suggestion that you discuss ways to change for the sake of the children. Start with the issue of swearing. Children model parents. How shocking it is for little boys to be spewing out foul language. Let your husband know that filthy stories hurt and embarrass you. If he tries to improve, encourage him and thank him. If he becomes more abusive, confront him again, with your pastor or helpful family friends available to discuss this serious problem.

You are not the first to write me about this problem. How do you know if you are being victimized? It seems abuse would be obvious, especially to the victim, but if you grew up in an alcoholic home, saw physical violence all around you, or were sexually abused, you will tolerate behavior and language that a woman coming from a more wholesome background would not accept.

Each day women share their stories with me and ask, "Is that abuse?" We all know black from white and know if we are being beaten black and blue. We also know if we have a model husband who treats us like a queen, never insults or demeans us, and has **125** never lifted a finger to harm us. We can all grasp the extremes, but what about that gray, murky area in the middle?

It often helps to have an outside perspective. We can all see someone else's victimization better than our own. We must also realize that the victimizer often accompanies his abuse with expressions such as "It's because I love you," "It's for your own good," or "It's God's will." And it happens in both non-Christian and Christian homes. The difference between a worldly abuser and a Christian one is only that the Christian has a verse to back up his actions.

Get some outside counsel yourself, then confront your husband.

Dear Florence:

I've never understood why any decent person would abuse anyone. Can't they see what they are doing? I teach a Bible study, and so many of the women have abusive husbands. Can you give me some understanding of the abuser's reasons? I guess I am one of those lucky ones who had a good home and now have a good husband.

Lucky in Lugonia

Dear Lucky:

You are indeed fortunate. I remember when I was teaching Bible studies and had women giving me their problems to solve. Remember that they had these difficulties before you met them and they will probably still have them when they move away. You are not single-handedly responsible for each life, yet you want to deal with each one to the best of your ability. Here is a list of explanations for an abuser's behavior with some information to help you assess the situation:

- The abusive person was likely abused himself as a child.
- The abuser tends to abuse in the same way he was violated. If he was beaten, he beats. If he was sexually molested, he molests. If he was verbally abused, he degrades and insults.
- The abuse is usually compulsive behavior, so good intentions, vows, prayers of repentance, and even threats of jail won't necessarily keep him from repeating the offense.
- The abuse probably won't just stop because he is getting older or going to church more. When I ask many women why they

allowed the abuse to go on, they tell me they thought their husband would see the error of his ways and change. Seldom is this true.

- The abuser may not see what he's doing as abusive. If he lived with abuse growing up, it seems natural to him. He has no doubt rationalized his behavior as necessary to keep the family under control.
- Power and control are the major motivations for abuse. The abuser, a victim himself, is scared to death he will lose control.

The best thing you can do for these women is agree with them that the behavior is abuse and help them get counseling that will work with the whole family. Don't just say, "Pray about it and the problem will disappear."

Types of Nonphysical, Nonsexual Abuse

Dear Florence:

I have read a lot about physical and sexual abuse, but I know there is abuse that doesn't fit these categories. When I ask friends who are being abused if it started at the beginning they tell me their husbands weren't bad men at the beginning, but that they worked up to it. What does this mean? Does abuse begin simply and then get worse? Are there other categories of abuse? I'm not married yet, but I want to know what to look out for.

Checking Up in Chattanooga

Dear Checking:

It's never too early to learn about what constitutes abuse so you can avoid it. So many women today—fine Christian women—are living in difficult situations that are leading toward abuse. Let's look at four kinds of abuse that begin in nonviolent ways: *intimidation, humiliation, deprivation,* and *isolation.*

Intimidation

Intimidation is defined as making someone timid, fearful, or frightened so they are compelled or controlled by threats. If you are afraid your husband will "let you have it" if you do something **127** wrong, you are being abused. The something wrong could be as simple as not picking up the shirts from the laundry, not getting home when you said you would, or buying a new book. Your action is not the problem; it just gives an abusive husband justification for the abuse he was going to heap on you anyway. He may threaten, "If you don't do what I say . . ." or "I won't tolerate . . ." or "You are pushing me . . ." When you live in genuine fear of making a mistake, you are suffering emotional abuse.

Several women I know personally were threatened for years by husbands who used guns as an intimidation tool. One woman was forced to sleep with a revolver under her pillow as a means to "remember who's in charge." Another slept with a shotgun between her and her husband. One dear lady in Canada who was on the verge of a nervous breakdown told me, "If I tried to head for the border, he'd have his men there to shoot me." All of these men were Christians. The first two situations, where guns were brought into the bed, ended in divorce. The men are still regarded as church leaders while the women, who never really told their stories, had to leave town. The Canadian woman is still living in daily fear for her life. Legally there was nothing any of these wives could do because they weren't actually shot. Police don't have time for hypothetical situations.

Living in life-threatening situations is abuse by *intimidation*.

Humiliation

Humiliation is lowering a person in someone else's eyes to mortify or abase them. When we were children, we often felt our parents were humiliating us if they showed up at school wearing an outfit we didn't like, if they sneezed during a program, or if they told a story about us to our peers. We would cry, "How *could* you!" The humiliation we are looking at here is of a far more serious nature.

Fred and I visited a couple's home for dinner. We didn't know them, but they were our hosts for a weekend conference. As soon as we arrived, the husband began pointing out his wife's faults. "She's late with dinner, but that's nothing new." "She always burns the rolls, so why does this surprise me?" He went on and on with these demeaning comments, expecting us to lower our view of her. Instead, we lowered our view of him as he humiliated his wife.

Some men humiliate their wives' clothes or appearance. Upon entering a party they might remark, "Look at how beautiful those other women are dressed. You never seem to wear the right thing." There's a comment designed to ruin an evening before it even gets started. At the dinner table a husband's comment, "Don't give her any dessert, she's too fat already," makes a wife want to hide under the table.

Fred and I met a young lady who was pulling herself together after an insulting divorce. Her husband was a Christian singer who was a charmer on stage. When he would bring her out, however, he would insult her in a way he thought was funny. Over time his jokes got worse, and she no longer wanted to go. He told her she was ruining his career and that if she stayed home, he'd lock her up so she couldn't go out with other men. He physically forced her into a closet and locked it before he went out for the night. "Why did you let him do this to you?" I asked. "By the time he locked me up I was so broken from his constant humiliation, I didn't think I deserved anything better," came her reply.

Constant put-downs, insults, and derogatory statements can wear women down to the point where they lose all feelings of worth or sense of identity. The one who takes sadistic joy in humiliating others is an insecure person who feels that by belittling others he will feel better about himself.

Humiliation of others is verbal abuse.

Deprivation

Deprivation is withholding something from another that they need or deserve. In the extreme, it's to withhold something until a person is too weak to fight for their rights. One of the most effective tools religious cults use to pull people into their clutches is deprivation. As the leaders are comfortably ensconced, they keep the converts in spartan quarters, deprived of sleep, food, and social contact until they are willing to be obedient. Christians are appalled at this, but we don't realize how many of our Christian families are being controlled in a similar manner. I talk with women who turn over their paychecks to husbands who control every cent and give them nothing or only a small allowance. Some women must account on paper for every cent they spend, and others must call their husbands from the store to get permission to buy a needed household item. I also know women who aren't allowed a credit card or checking account, women whose husbands do the shopping to control food purchases, and women who have no car and are at the mercy of others for transportation.

Two young sisters came to me for help with their eating disorders. As we talked, I learned that their father put a high priority on being slim. He controlled their eating and when he found they sneaked food, he punished them by taking away all their clothes except two school dresses. He told them what weight they should be and would not give them any more clothes until they got to that weight. As a result one became anorexic and the other bulimic. The mother was so emotionally abused herself that she had long since given up any hint of influence. The father, a Bible-toting elder in the church, was so impressed with the girls' weight loss that he stood up at prayer meeting and suggested this method to other families with chubby daughters.

Dawn was steeped in saintly submission as a young bride and right from the beginning did whatever Mason told her to do. He handled all the money and gave her nothing, saying, "As long as you go everywhere with me you don't need any money to squander." They opened a small ice cream shop together and at first they worked side by side. Once the business stabilized, though, Mason assigned Dawn to work six full days a week while he supervised occasionally. Mason bought new sport coats and bright ties and seemed always ready to take off at any time with anybody who dropped by. He decided that Dawn and the other clerks should wear uniforms, so six days a week Dawn was in khaki slacks and an orange polo shirt. When Dawn looked in Mason's closet one day, she began to cry. When Mason came in to see what was wrong she told him, "You have all these nice clothes, and all I have is khaki slacks and orange shirts and two church dresses." Mason looked surprised. "But you don't need any clothes," he said. "You don't do anything but work." How true!

A sad-looking lady in a drab dress waited until everyone had left the church before she came up to ask me her question. "I've been sick for almost a year and my husband won't let me go to the doctor. He says he loves me so much he doesn't want any other man to touch me. Do you think that's the truth?" When I asked her what she thought, she tearfully replied, "I think he's hoping I'll die."

This poor lady sobbed as she sank into the front pew. During the next half-hour she told me a litany of emotionally abusive tricks her husband had conceived over their years of marriage. At the time she had not seen them as abusive but as her duty as a submissive wife; however, when we looked at the pattern objectively, she could see his manipulation as abuse.

Willful *deprivation* is abuse.

Isolation

Isolation is the act of separating a person from others (e.g., quarantine). One of the most subtle but serious forms of nonviolent abuse is isolating the wife and family from normal social relationships. Sometimes this is physical, moving the family to a remote area where there are few or no other people. Often a move is described as temporary, but it may last for years. Homes (trailers are the frequent choices for men isolating their families) often lack even the basic amenities of life and leave wives too ashamed to have friends in for coffee. Children are too far away from school to participate in extracurricular activities, or they are home-schooled, effectively eliminating social contact. Often there is no phone and no car, and the wife becomes a recluse in the name of submission.

Sometimes isolation doesn't appear to be this dismal. I've met women who lived in large houses, drove fine cars, and wore designer dresses but were not allowed to go anywhere or do anything without permission. People who didn't know envied them, but these women lived isolated, lonely lives. Often pious husbands convince wives they are too pure to be contaminated by friends **131** whose doctrine may be flawed or whose behavior is not exemplary. One pastor's wife told me that every time she found a friend she enjoyed in the church, her husband would in some way undermine the relationship. When it was broken, he would say, "See, she wasn't what she appeared to be. You're well rid of her."

Some abusive husbands manage to disrupt old friendships as well as new ones. Bev and Mary had been friends for years. Mary's husband abused her and the children, and after a long period of suffering, Mary left and got a divorce. Bev's husband, who had already moved her to a remote area in an attempt to isolate her, forbade her to see Mary anymore. "All divorced women run around, and I won't let you be tainted," he said. On his unfounded opinion a long-lasting friendship was broken for good, further isolating Bev and keeping her submissively dependent on her husband.

One young woman told me her husband moved her into a senior citizen trailer park so there wouldn't be any eligible men around she might get interested in. He said he was protecting her from temptation. Another's husband wouldn't let her wear attractive clothes; he kept her in high-necked white blouses lest men should lust after her.

Men who are sexually abusing their children usually don't let them go to other friends' houses for fear they'll talk. They claim it's for protection from others when there actually needs to be protection from them. They keep children in odd, out-of-date clothes that make them look strange, thereby isolating them from social relationships.

Abuse of any kind is a control issue, and isolation makes it easier to control. When you see a wimpy, saintly submissive wife with drab, docile children who look frightened, accompanied by a father who carries a Bible and praises the Lord, you may well be facing an abused and dysfunctional family.

Isolation, whether it's physical or emotional, can be abuse.

Why Do Women Stay in Abusive Situations?

Dear Florence:

Why do women stay in abusive situations? Are they not too smart to start with? I don't have much sympathy for those women who don't get their act together and leave an abusive husband. I believe we need to take charge of our lives and not let other people mess us up.

Taking Charge in Torrance

Dear Taking Charge:

I used to be like you. Because of my Choleric nature I thought people who didn't move to correct their problems were weak. That was until I'd worked with many abused women. Now I see that many have been slowly ground down to a point where they have no resistance. Many think this is their cross to bear. Some think they have no choice. Some have been told to continue to be submissive and that when they are sweet enough their husbands will change their behavior.

Once you become aware of the hopelessness of many hurting women, your attitude will be sympathetic. If a woman was abused as a child, she often feels helpless to do anything about her situation. Because of this background of trauma, she is less apt to see her situation as abusive and more apt to stay in it than an emotionally healthy woman would be. To help you understand why women don't take action in harmful situations, I've made a list of the reasons women have most frequently given to me.

____ 1. **No choice.** I have no options, no place to go, no one who cares, no money. I might as well grin and bear it.

____ 2. **Religious reasons.** As a Christian I must stay in this marriage and hope for rewards in heaven. I'm committed to obedience.

____ 3. **Children.** I'll take the abuse for the sake of the children. They need a stable home life and I can't disrupt them.

____ 4. **Finances.** I can't support myself and the children; I need his income to live. I'll just keep quiet and keep going.

____ 5. **Wifely duty.** I was taught that sex was what I had to do even though he's abusive. It's my cross to bear.

____ 6. **Social status.** Without his name I'd be nobody. I'd be out of the country club and ostracized by his friends.

____ 7. **The comfort zone.** It's easier to stay here where we're all settled than to uproot everyone. I guess I can stand it a little longer.

133

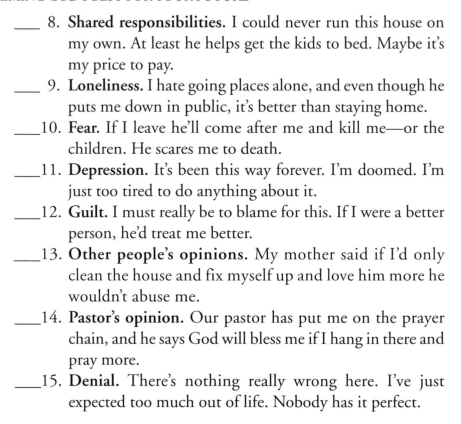

____ 8. **Shared responsibilities.** I could never run this house on my own. At least he helps get the kids to bed. Maybe it's my price to pay.

____ 9. **Loneliness.** I hate going places alone, and even though he puts me down in public, it's better than staying home.

____10. **Fear.** If I leave he'll come after me and kill me—or the children. He scares me to death.

____11. **Depression.** It's been this way forever. I'm doomed. I'm just too tired to do anything about it.

____12. **Guilt.** I must really be to blame for this. If I were a better person, he'd treat me better.

____13. **Other people's opinions.** My mother said if I'd only clean the house and fix myself up and love him more he wouldn't abuse me.

____14. **Pastor's opinion.** Our pastor has put me on the prayer chain, and he says God will bless me if I hang in there and pray more.

____15. **Denial.** There's nothing really wrong here. I've just expected too much out of life. Nobody has it perfect.

So many Christian women are convinced that being submissive includes accepting any kind of abuse forever. When they are suffering, many are afraid to go to their pastors for fear they won't be believed, or they expect that the pastor will look down on them when he hears of their abuse. Many women don't trust any men because of their victimization and they are especially afraid of an authority figure. Often their childhood abuser was viewed as a religious person, giving them doubt about religious figures and even about God himself.

Some Christian women don't take action because they feel if they pray hard enough the situation will change. Isaac Black, pastor, professor, and author of *Assault on God's Image,* states that abuse is a serious problem within the church and most of it is not reported until it becomes violent. "In addition, too many people in abusive situations have been told that it is their Christian duty to hang in there and suffer as a Christian, that it is their role to be faithful and willing to endure some hardship as a good soldier of Jesus Christ."[1]

Some women feel abuse is the "poorer" part of their vow "for richer or poorer." Some have even been told that the more they suffer on earth the bigger their reward will be in heaven. Some feel that if they hold on long enough, their children and Christian friends will rise up and call them blessed.

But God doesn't call us to submit to abuse of any kind.

We must be compassionately understanding of women in trouble of this kind, helping them find knowledgeable and caring counselors. Scripture urges us to "warn those who are idle, encourage the timid, help the weak, be patient with everyone" (1 Thess. 5:14 NIV). Those of us who wish to lift up such hurting people must, therefore, be full of wisdom and love.

Is Someone Taking Advantage of You?

Dear Florence:

I am in my forties and struggling to keep my obligations under control. My parents seem to have nothing to do and are demanding of my time. They feel I should drop everything when they call. My children are teens and need all kinds of help, from buying sports equipment to feeding friends. Some days I don't know which end is up and I feel everyone is taking advantage of me. Does anyone else feel this way?

Obliging in Ohio

Dear Obliging:

You are not alone! In fact, you are one of the millions trapped in what is being called the Sandwich Generation. You are sandwiched between your parents who want attention on one side and your children who demand assistance on the other. You can't win.

To keep your sanity you have to develop some boundaries on each side. Give your parents a set amount of times each week—every Tuesday for dinner, every Thursday morning for shopping, doctor's appointments—whatever you consider within reason. Explain that you are not feeling as peppy as you used to and that you have to get your life under control. Your children have great needs and you have to come up with a balance. Explain to your children how difficult it has become for you and try to gain additional job responsibility out of them for every new task they ask of you. Don't let both sides squeeze you until there is no filling left in the sandwich.

Ministering Too Well for Too Long

As Christian women, we want to care for others, always be kind, and have the attitude of a servant. Our aim is to become like Christ, so we give freely, feeding the sick and offering water to the thirsty. But some of us minister too well for too long. Because of our good nature, people take advantage of us. As exemplary wives, some of us become submissive to the point of stupidity. As loving mothers, some of us become maids and chauffeurs to our children who easily expect too much from us. As adult children, we allow our parents to usurp our authority and drain our energy.

So many people I talk with have at least one of these problems; some are mired down with people dragging on them from every angle. In his book, *Rejection Junkies,* Dr. Gary Lawrence of New Life Dynamic Christian Counseling Center in Phoenix, Arizona, calls these people "emotional energy thieves." We have to ask ourselves when a giving spirit turns into martyrdom. Have we somehow crossed the line of rational reason and don't know how to get back? Get rid of your false guilt, figure out what you can handle, explain your limits to the family, and don't be the sandwich any longer.

Boomerang Children

Dear Florence:

I have been a good, dutiful mother, and now my children are all out of the house. My daughter is divorced and she keeps begging me to let her come live with us until she can get her life together. She has two little girls who are adorable, but I don't want them underfoot all the time in our small home. I've waited all my married life to have this house to myself. Have you dealt with this problem before, and do you have any suggestions in case she does end up moving in? Thank you.

Alone in Abilene

Dear Alone:

You have a problem that is growing because of the divorce rate and the number of adult children unable to financially support themselves. I will answer your question by sharing with you the story of my friend Jane and the list of suggestions we came up with to help this type of situation.

Jane was the perfect superwoman to her family and friends. When you needed help you went to Jane. She was an exemplary mother and we all praised her dedication and endless energy. She was a Choleric with all her friends, but seemed to be taken advantage of at home. She had the idea that to be the good wife and mother she had to wait on everyone. Everything she did was better than what any of her friends seemed to master. She and her husband, Will, raised three children to be productive adults. All got married and moved out of the house. Finally Jane and Will had some time to themselves. It was fun to travel a little in their motor home and come back to a house that was as neat as it had been when they left. Jane redecorated the living and dining areas and even dared put in off-white carpeting, which brightened up the whole house and made it seem more expansive. Jane's friends who still had children at home were envious of her freedom and opportunities. "I can hardly wait!" they often said.

But Jane's carefree days didn't last long. They ended the day her oldest daughter, Roxie, called to say she was divorcing her husband and was going to marry Greg as soon as her divorce was final.

"How could she do this to the family?" Jane questioned. "And who is Greg anyway?"

Roxie never asked her mother's opinion, however, and before Jane knew it the old husband was gone and a new one was in. Jane resented the switch but kept her feelings to herself. Greg was the tall, lanky, cool type. Roxie thought he looked like Clint Eastwood **139** although Jane couldn't see any resemblance at all. From her perspective he was dull and a little on the lazy side. Choleric Roxie had always been the domineering type and she seemed to enjoy pushing Phlegmatic Greg around. He just smiled, sighed, and did what she said.

Will thought his first daughter could do no harm, and he rationalized the divorce quickly. Roxie and Greg sold the house she had lived in with her former husband, hoping to get enough money to put a down payment on a new one. However, when the figures were totaled they found they had just enough money to pay off the accumulated debts they'd each brought into the marriage. There was nothing left, not even enough for a deposit on a decent apartment.

As stark reality overcame romance in this new marriage, the couple found themselves with no place to stay. Roxie called Jane and Will, who were on a trip to Alaska, and asked if she and Greg could stay at their house while they were away. Will immediately approved the plan although Jane was skeptical of this invasion. Will made her feel selfish and materialistic about her hesitancy, so she gave in. After all, wasn't she the sweet, submissive wife? And wasn't this her daughter in need?

Jane assumed Roxie and Greg would live in Roxie's former bedroom, but when she came home three weeks later she found the couple firmly entrenched in the master bedroom. Jane was shocked that this new man was in her bed, but Will calmed her down and suggested that she and he live in the motor home in the driveway and let the young people have the room. Once again Jane was made to feel selfish when she balked, so she gave in.

When she told me this story later, she got red in the face. "Roxie and Clint Eastwood were in my house, in my room, in my bed, and I was sleeping in the driveway!"

Will, who had just retired, suggested they take a lot of trips and "leave the kids the house while we're gone." In the next year while the kids took over Jane's house, Will and Jane crossed the country and back, looking for places to go and canyons to see. In that one year they were home only twenty-one days. But even in that short time it was quite apparent that Greg rarely worked. By the time Jane attempted to reclaim her territory, Roxie was pregnant—and angry.

"We can't throw her out now," Will explained. "We don't want to be the bad guys." And they weren't. Roxie and Greg were the bad guys. Roxie, with her hot Choleric temper, was in control of the house and no one dared cross her for fear of bearing the brunt of her anger.

Greg reacted in typical Phlegmatic fashion. He withdrew, took to Will's recliner, built a wall around himself, and watched TV.

Roxie reprimanded Jane if she laid her jacket on a chair or left a glass on the kitchen counter. Roxie liked all surfaces to be neat, but she had no interest in cleaning below the surface. That was up to Jane to do.

Will and Jane consoled themselves, believing that after the baby was born Roxie and Greg would move out. Surely they'd want their own place then. While they waited, Will and Jane took more trips and were shocked when they found the baby was to be born in their bed rather than in a hospital. Jane would never have thought of Roxie's having a baby at home—especially in *her* bed.

While Will and Jane were staring blankly at the red rocks of Sedona, they received news of little Jason's birth. They tried to get excited as they drove home to see the new addition to the family, but they couldn't help thinking about the consequences of Roxie's decision to quit her job to be a "real mother." Greg was still working only sporadically in part-time jobs and had developed no feeling of responsibility.

Will explained to Jane, "We can hardly throw our little girl out on the street at a time like this." Or at any other time it seemed. So Will and Jane went on another trip to Calgary to see the annual stampede. Jane told me, "I hoped to get killed by the rampaging bulls."

When they returned home, they were greeted with the news that their daughter was pregnant again. She was also sick, so Jane became the nurse, baby-sitter, and cleaning lady. Relationships deteriorated during that time, and Will played a lot of golf. Roxie didn't like Jane and Will to turn up their TV too loud or to have **141** company in the house; it interfered with her rest or infringed on her privacy.

By the time the second baby was born, Jane was ready to scream. While Roxie was giving birth in the hospital—not in Jane's bed this time—Jane moved Roxie's things into the guest room where she and Will had been sleeping.

She bought a new mattress and sheets and put a lock on her bedroom door. Then Jane took a real look at her house. There were spots on the off-white carpeting, crayon marks on the newly papered walls, and pink magic-marker scribbles on her toilet seat. There were teeth marks on her lipsticks, rips in her towels, and crumbs between the cushions of the couch.

When Jane told Greg she didn't like the way they let little Jason run wild, he replied, "Well, Roxie really doesn't like living here."

That did it. Jane was ready to explode. She wanted to shout, "Doesn't like living here? How does she think I like it?" But once more she bit her tongue and said nothing.

That weekend Will and Jane took off for the desert, and when they had settled into a trailer park for the evening, Jane tried to explain that she could not live this way any longer. When Will once again retorted, "We can't throw them out with a new baby!" Jane yelled, "You just don't get it, do you?"

Will was shocked at her response, but not as shocked as he was fifteen minutes later when Jane emerged from the back of the motor home and brushed by him carrying a suitcase. She stopped at the door and gave a little farewell speech. "I am leaving you. If you ever decide I'm of more value to you than our children are, you may come after me."

By the time Will pulled himself together and got in the car to follow her, Jane was walking out the gate of the trailer park, trudging along with her suitcase in her hand.

"I love you more than I love them," Will called out to her. "I guess I didn't know it bothered you that much."

He just didn't get it. But he wanted to. They went back and talked for three hours, reviewing every step of what had happened and how it had gotten so out of hand that Jane felt like an intruder in her own house.

Once they agreed on what to do, they returned and met with Roxie and Greg. They simply stated they felt it was time for the couple to get their own place and they would expect them out in two weeks. Much to Jane's amazement the couple accepted the news positively, and within two weeks Greg had found a better job, Roxie was rehired at the old job she had left, Greg's mother took on the full-time baby-sitting, and they were thrilled to be in a place of their own.

Jane could hardly wait to clean out the house and start life all over again. When I asked her what she would do if she were ever in that position again, she laughed and said, "They'd have to lock me up."

So I rephrased my question: "What advice could you give to someone whose adult children might return?" She thought about it a while, then she and I came up with the following guidelines:

1. **Be in agreement.** Before you take anyone into your home, agree with your mate that you will stand together on decisions. Jane realizes that their daughter manipulated her father and caused a division between her and Will. If agreement doesn't come instantly, there at least must be unity and a willingness to talk over the issues privately. If one partner is strongly opposed to the return of this adult child, with or without a family, it will never work, and it could cause marital chaos. It would be better to put them up in a motel for a short time than allow them to move in.

2. **Establish control.** If it is agreed that they may come into your home, it must be made clear to them whose home it is, and if they show the first sign of bucking for control, both parents must take quick action. Once they found the couple in their bedroom, Will should have backed Jane up and immediately moved Roxie and Greg to another room. He should not have allowed the daughter to dictate the volume on the TV or decide when they could have company. If you are dealing with this type of situation alone, without a mate, you must still take a stand and be firm in your decisions. Perhaps you could bring in a sibling to support you. And even though **143**

the disciplining of your grandchildren is basically their parents' problem, when they live with you, you must establish what's acceptable behavior. Remember, if it's your china they're breaking, you have a right to speak up.

3. **Set a time limit right from the start.** Don't let anyone move in for an indefinite time. Roxie and Greg lived in Jane's house for four years. Each time Jane was ready to make them leave, there would either be a financial crisis or a new baby on the way, making her look like a heartless grandmother. If Roxie and Greg had known this invasion had to terminate in one month, they might have hustled a little harder to get their finances in order and find a Plan B!

4. **Assign jobs.** Make it clear from the beginning that you are not slave labor. Sit down with the boarder and establish who does what. Don't start doing their laundry and making their bed. Put the responsibility on the right set of shoulders. You have already raised your family once; you don't need to do it again a second time. Jane got no credit for all she did; in fact, she was criticized for how and when she did it!

5. **Keep your regular mealtimes.** If the guests want to eat at separate times or don't like what you cook, make it clear they can buy their own food, cook it and clean up from it. I know one mother who bought a secondhand refrigerator and put it in the garage. Her son was responsible to stock it and eat from it. He was not to deplete her supplies. If he wished to eat with the family, he was to tell her ahead of time and be there on time.

6. **Let them know this is not a hotel.** Not only should meal times be established and clean-up assigned, but guests must not expect hotel services. You should not be in charge of their business calls, their dry cleaning, or their change of linens. The minute any requests like this are made, tell them firmly, "We have no staff for that. This is not a hotel."

7. **Make them contribute financially.** Granting family members a week or two of hospitality can be considered a kind maternal gift, but if there are signs that this visit will be longer, establish a time frame and ask them to share the expenses.

They can either pay rent or cover some of the utilities, but this contribution, even if it is small, helps them to keep in touch with the expenses of running a home. Do not let them take you for granted or they'll never leave! We once had guests who ran up huge phone bills and were affronted when asked to pay their share of the charges.

8. **Don't let them criticize.** Right from the start let these needy people know that if they don't like your home, your lifestyle, or your friends, they can leave. Sometimes when adult children move home, they feel like a failure and they may take out their anger on you. But you are not their problem. If they had handled their own lives better they probably wouldn't be back. Don't let them make you the target of their misplaced anger.

9. **Don't use the children as a dumping ground.** Often when grandchildren move in with Grandma and Grandpa, the grandparents drop on them the feelings they don't dare say to the parents. "When is your mother going to grow up, stop smoking, dress better, fix her hair, and get a decent job?" These comments may seem harmless to adults but they place adult responsibility on children. Then the little ones feel they have to do something about the complaints, yet they have no clout with which to do it. They think they are failing you if they can't get Mother to change. Similarly, if there's been a divorce, don't review how rotten the in-law parent is. Don't tell the children if their father were a decent provider they wouldn't all be crowded into your house. The children are confused enough. Don't dump your anger on them.

10. **Don't assume guilt.** Jane felt she had really matured when she was able to face her daughter and not feel guilty. Roxie complained when Jane didn't always want to baby-sit so she and Greg could go out more. Jane stated calmly but clearly, "I did not have these babies; you did. I love them, but I am not responsible for their care. When I do baby-sit it is a gift of love to you." Jane was so proud of herself when she told me, "I'm not going to carry her guilt any longer." **145**

11. **Relax and try to enjoy this time.** This is the graduate school of motherhood. Once you make the rules, see that they are followed; then have fun with the family so they remember their time at Grandma's as a positive experience.

Roxie told one of Jane's friends, "Mother's gotten a lot nicer since we moved out."

Mothering Too Well

Dear Florence:

I am a single parent who has struggled to raise a son. He still wants me to support him and I'm afraid if I give him too much he will never get a job. He seems happy to stay at home and play computer games, but I feel he should grow up and support himself. He's now twenty-one. When should I force him to go to work? My friends say as long as he's good and doesn't give me any trouble I shouldn't push him. What do you think?

Good Mother in Grand Mesa

Dear Good Mother:

You are doing your son no favor by letting him enjoy an indolent life. You are helping him believe the world owes him a living, which will cripple his ability to survive on his own and prevent him from becoming the man the Lord intended him to be. He needs to grow up and become responsible for his own support. I don't know your financial ability, but I can share a similar story about Charlene that might help you see the folly of being too good a mother.

Charlene asked to see me after I spoke at a women's retreat. She was very upset about her son, who never seemed to hold a job very long. She wanted to know what she could do to help him become more stable.

As Charlene shared her story with me, she explained that her husband had left when her son was quite young. She had worked hard as a professional to support herself and her son, and she had managed quite well. She had even saved up a healthy retirement fund. She paid for her son's college education, but in spite of his training he never seemed able to hold a job for very long. He was always trying new business ventures that used up any money he acquired. When he was deeply in debt because of overspending on credit cards, Charlene bailed him out.

Then he got the "financial chance of a lifetime" to invest in a business with a friend, but Charlene's son had no money. When she refused to loan it to him, he badgered her, made her feel guilty, and actually threatened her physically. So, being the good mother that she was, she finally gave in and borrowed against her retirement fund so he could invest in this business venture. The business failed and the bill collectors started coming to Charlene's door. She paid off what she could until her retirement fund was completely gone.

When her son's car was repossessed, he convinced Charlene to let him drive her car. One morning he took her to her office, promising to pick her up that evening. Charlene waited and waited, but her son never came. She actually spent the night at the office without anything to eat. The next morning, she was ashamed to admit to her coworkers that she had slept on the floor all night, but it was even more humiliating to admit to them that her son had actually stripped her of her car, her money, and her retirement fund.

I helped Charlene see that her son's having to grow up without a father and the early struggles they'd had financially did not justify her son's taking advantage of her now. I encouraged her to insist that he take responsibility for himself and not give in to the guilt he tried to impose on her. Charlene followed my instructions and stopped protecting her son from the difficulties of the real world. Then she could start taking care of herself again.

It took some hard lessons, but Charlene finally took charge of her situation.

Fairness and Honesty

Dear Florence:

My son is home from college and has his first job. My husband feels we should charge him rent so he will learn to become responsible. I have trouble asking our own son to pay me when we don't need the money. I like to give my children everything they need.

Generous from Georgia

Dear Generous:

I have a great suggestion for you from a family who handled a similar situation creatively.

The Johnsons told me how they handled their son when he came back from college and had his first job. He wanted to be independent and yet live at home for a while. First, his mother went with him to look at a few inexpensive apartments. They were all in poor neighborhoods and he didn't like any of them. She took the amount of money of the lowest rent, cut it in half, and charged him that much for one room and bath with kitchen privileges. He didn't have to join his parents for dinner, but if he did want to eat with them he was to call and let her know. She also told him that when he got his first raise his rent would go up proportionately.

Sometimes as he paid his rent he would grumble about having to give money to his mother, but she referred back to their arrangement and suggested he could look at one of those apartments again. By the end of two years the young man was doing well enough to rent a decent apartment. He left with positive feelings that his parents had been fair and honest with him. What he didn't know was that they had deposited all of his rent money in an account for him and when he left they gave him the sum with interest.

He was dumbfounded and apologized for the times he had complained. These parents handled the situation well, made the standards clear from the beginning, and helped him see that it costs money to live. They could have let him have everything for free and hoped for eternal gratitude in return; instead they charged him fairly, taught him some lessons, and saved him money he would probably not have amassed himself. The Johnsons did it right!

Instead of a farewell with hard feelings, the son left excited about the challenges ahead. He is often heard starting a conversation with, "Wait 'til I tell you what my parents did for me!"

Parenting Our Parents

Dear Florence:

From the time I was a child I have been taking care of people. I sensed early on that my mother needed me and I made her decisions and chose her clothes when I was surely too young to be doing that. As an adult, I still have people looking up to me for advice. I find that I can give a quick answer to people I meet in a restaurant. My mother is elderly and I'm still running her life. Are there any cautions for people like me. Why am I like this?

Ann Landers Junior in Ann Arbor

Dear Ann:

I understand your question because I'm much like you. I took over for my mother when I was four and my first brother was born. You and I are Choleric personalities who by nature take control of our own lives and the lives of anyone around us who seems to be incompetent. This is not a well-accepted trait at times, but we get into it without thinking. When I stand in the dress department of Macy's, women ask me if I can find this dress in their size. In airports they ask me when the plane will leave, and in hospitals I seem to become a nurse.

Many of us who, at an early age, were put in the position of mothering our mothers grew up needing to be in control. With this tendency we very easily become the stability for codependents searching for a solid rock.

I look back on my adult life and see how I have repeatedly been the positive person picking up the people with pitiful pasts. Before I understood victimization, I didn't know why so many sad souls attached themselves to me. Now I realize that someone who was abused as a child seeks out adults who seem to have their lives under control to offer a measure of protection. They are still looking for a mother—someone to care for them—and I seem to fit the image. There is nothing wrong with uplifting others, but we need to see what it is we are doing and why we are doing it. I realize now that I gathered pain-filled people as if I were stringing them into a strand of beads.

149

Now I am able to listen to the presenting problem, pull out the probable truth, suggest books, tapes, or counseling, and not have the string of beads strangle me.

I'm not alone in my sometimes overwhelming feelings of responsibility. Thousands of women (and some men) were programmed this way during their childhood. We have felt compelled to bear responsibility for every oppressed woman in America (or every unhappy person in your family). And while we are saving the world, we are often sacrificing close personal relationships. As a result it could be lonely for us in the old ladies home when the world forgets to visit.

Those of us who lost much of our childhood in mothering Mother need to take an especially sharp look at our caretaking nature and make sure we're not gathering up too many beads that will sooner or later make us choke. And even if we did not have to mother our mothers when we were children, we may well find ourselves in that role as our mothers' increasing age and health problems reduce their independence.

The time comes when instead of them caring for us, we may have to care for our parents. As you asked, there are some emotional precautions we should consider.

One of the things I learned through my own experience is to make sure there is no guilt on your part that will hang on and drain you emotionally long after the parent is gone. I remembered one uncalled-for comment I snapped at my mother. I knew I should have been more patient and I knew she had done nothing wrong, but I didn't say I was sorry. She died shortly thereafter and even though I've confessed it to the Lord, I still think of that day each time I drive by the convalescent home where she died. Why didn't I say I was sorry? How important it is for each one of us to clear up any unfinished apologies before it's too late.

I recently received a letter from my childhood friend, Peggy. She had married Roger while I was at college and had children before I was even married. She and Roger looked like the perfect couple, but he had emotional problems and ultimately deserted her and their four children. He showed no signs of responsibility, and Peggy and the children worked hard to keep their lives together. I've kept in touch over the years, and she wrote to tell me that Roger had been ill. When it appeared he was dying, she sent for the children to all meet at the hospital. They didn't want to come because he had never been there for them, but at Peggy's pleading they came from far away. She told me that as they stood around the bed together each one told their father that they forgave him. Although he couldn't talk, he squeezed each hand, letting them know he heard. Peggy said it was the most cleansing experience for the family, a time they will never forget. No matter how we feel people have treated us, we must forgive them and remove any future guilt from our minds.

Dear Florence:

My mother is no longer able to care for herself and the solution of how to care for her is on my sisters and me. I think some of my sisters think that if they take her in they will get everything Mother owns. I don't need any of her things and only hope I'll get back the ring I gave her. How do we make these decisions?

Undecided in Urbana

Dear Undecided:

You are wise to think about this situation carefully and discuss it honestly with your sisters. Sometimes we have no choice about what we have to do when our parents are no longer able to live independently. At other times, when there are several siblings, for instance, there are various possibilities. One decision is whether you will move the dependent parent into your home.

The right reason for bringing a parent into your home or under your care is to provide the most positive environment you can for his or her waning years. One sister may have a larger house, one may have no children at home, or one may have more money available for the parent's care. These are valid reasons.

The wrong reasons for supporting a parent are thinking you'll get points from the family for how noble you are, still trying to win the affirmation from this parent that you've never received, or thinking you'll get more in the will than those siblings who have done

151

nothing. Unfortunately, these hopes, subconscious though they may be, don't often come true. Instead, exhausted and frustrated, you could end up with no credit, no affirmation, and no money.

An example of this is Claire, who came to me in a state of disbelief. "My mother is suing me!" she exclaimed. "I'm in a state of shock!" I could hardly imagine it myself.

Claire grew up with an alcoholic mother who produced thirteen children, only four of whom were still alive. The son had divorced himself from the remaining family, and the three daughters had stayed somewhat close to the mother. Of these three, Claire and Faye had led relatively stable lives while Sara has been labeled schizophrenic. The burden of caring for their mother had fallen on Claire, who was still subconsciously hoping to get her mother's approval.

"I've done everything I could for her," she explained to me. "I've bought her groceries, prescriptions, and clothes. And she never even says thank you. One day I asked her if she could reimburse me for some of the month's food and she said, 'I only have six dollars, but if you want to take the last cent a poor old lady has, go ahead.'"

Claire started to cry at the sick control her mother had over her. "I've given my all. I've done my best, and that's all I get from her."

But there was worse to come.

Mother never seemed to have any money, even though she had Social Security and a hundred dollars a month from renting out the little family house she still owned. Claire had made arrangements for her mother to live in senior-citizen housing, but to qualify for the low-income program she could not own property. It was suggested that the mother quickly quit-claim the house to the four living children, and Claire took care of all the details and did the legwork. Once the transaction was in process, Sara sensed she might have inherited the house herself if Claire hadn't split it four ways. She decided she wanted it.

Without any understanding of how long it had taken Claire to get their mother into the housing program and what legal circumstances were involved, Sara marched in without warning, removed Mother from the senior-citizens complex, and brought her to her house. When Claire went to visit her at the complex, she was gone and there was a bill for five hundred dollars that Claire had to pay. Sara got Mother to stop the process of the quit-claim, take the house back, will it to Sara, and then sue Claire for fraud and mental stress.

The day Claire received the summons she was flabbergasted. Why would Mother sue her after all she'd done for her? When Claire poured this out to me, she explained that the house was worth at most $30,000 and it was "such a pit" full of bad memories that she didn't want any part of it. She had done all she could to help her mother and for her efforts she was accused of stealing one-fourth of an old house.

As time went on, Claire spent six thousand dollars on legal fees to defend herself against her mother's charges and ultimately the judge threw out the case. Mother got the house but ended up with lawyers' bills, a lien on the house, and a fine from the housing program for lying about the ownership.

A few weeks later Sara called Claire and said, "Thanks to you, Mother is having a terrible Mother's Day."

"That's when I realized I had to wake up. My mother had never appreciated anything I had done. I ended up being the bad guy and the one sister who caused the problems is getting the house."

Later, when Sara was sick of living with her mother, she had her call Claire and ask to move in with her. "I hope there's no hard feelings," Mother said.

Claire felt she had finally grown up when she was able to say, "No, Sara took you out of the place I had you in and she is now responsible for your welfare. You and she can work it out. I refuse to take the blame anymore."

Most of us will not be sued by our mothers, but we should guard ourselves from being put in any position where our emotional expectations will be dashed. Anytime we expect credit for family favors, we open ourselves up for disappointments. Anytime we expect our mothers or fathers to change their habit patterns and begin to praise us because they're getting old, we become the hurt little child again. We must do what we know is right, expecting nothing in return and being grateful for any thanks we may receive.

Dear Florence:

I have two elderly parents who are in good health and able to care for each other. My problem is my mother wants me with her night and day, and if I don't run when she calls, she pouts for days and sometimes feigns sickness. My family needs my attention more than Mother does. Do I have a right to say no and still be a good Christian daughter?

Pulled in Pomona

Dear Pulled:

Our Christian duty is to see that our parents are properly cared for, not left without the necessities. It is expected that to the best of our ability we spend time with them and include them in family holidays and celebrations when possible. It sounds to me as if your mother has had a hold over you for years and she has gotten more possessive as the years have gone by. You cannot be manipulated into doing her every whim and then feeling guilty when you can't obey. Listen to Chelsea's story. This friend of mine learned how to handle a similar situation.

Chelsea was an only child who was reared by a very domineering, Choleric mother and a Phlegmatic father. Often when we think of only children, we assume they will be very self-centered and used to getting their own way, but this was not true in Chelsea's case. In her family everything centered on Chelsea's mother.

When Chelsea married and moved to another state, friends predicted she would be homesick; they doubted she would survive without her mother. Much to their surprise, Chelsea survived very well. She began to think for herself and learned to acknowledge her own personal feelings. She reared her children to be quite independent, yet they have a good relationship with her.

All was going well until Chelsea's parents retired and moved to Chelsea's town. At first it was nice that Chelsea's mom wanted to cook each evening for Chelsea, her husband, Joe, and their children. After all, they had very busy schedules and reasoned it would "help Mom feel useful while she adjusted to her new surroundings." Then the phone calls started every morning, just like a wake-up call, and they continued frequently through the day. Chelsea

154

began to long for the freedom she had enjoyed before her parents moved to town. But how do you break a pattern when the other person doesn't want to break it?

At first when Chelsea would suggest they shouldn't eat together quite so much, her mother would become sad and teary-eyed and say, "I guess we should have stayed in New York. At least people had time for us there." If Chelsea let the answering machine take the early-morning calls, mother would leave messages that hinted at tears or implied that there was an emergency. Then Chelsea would feel guilty and worry, *Perhaps one of them is sick. What if they really need me?*

As Chelsea spent many hours in prayer over this situation, God began to show her how enmeshed she had become with her mother as a child and how controlling her mother really was. She remembered the times her mother had manipulated her until she was willing to think and behave the way her mother wanted her to.

One day as she was praying, she saw that her mother held her in emotional bondage. In her mind Chelsea saw her mother's manipulation wrapped around her just like chains. Then she saw her mother standing between her and Jesus, and Chelsea realized her mother had actually become a barrier to her spiritual growth. She said, "Lord, how do I get rid of this emotional bondage?"

In Chelsea's mind the Lord said, "Just flex your muscles. You are strong, and you can do it."

Chelsea pictured herself taking a deep breath and flexing her muscles. As she did, the chains fell at her feet. However, in her mental picture, her mother was still standing between Chelsea and Jesus. Chelsea said, "Jesus, how do I get past my mother to you?"

Jesus let her see that all she had to do was reach for him. In her mental picture, as she reached for Jesus, her hand went right through her mother to Jesus as though her mother were a vapor. Chelsea told me, "Florence, it was then I realized my mother had taught me her happiness was more important than anything else and that I was a bad girl if I didn't keep her happy. When Jesus gave me that picture, I realized I had been manipulated by my mother most of my life, and it was up to me to stop the manipulation. I just had to flex my muscles."

155

"Flexing her muscles" has been a difficult process, but Chelsea has begun to set some guidelines on how often she has meals with her parents. Mother was not pleased at first, and sometimes she still threatens to move back to New York, but Chelsea is not swayed by those threats now. She keeps focused on making decisions that will be best for her and her family. The phone calls still come early each morning, but Chelsea doesn't feel obligated to answer them. She lets the answering machine take them if the timing isn't good, and she calls her mother back later.

As she has begun to heal, Chelsea has come to realize her mother never looked at her as a separate entity. She didn't affirm her as a person. This became obvious recently when Chelsea made a statement to her mother that was completely provable: "It's raining outside." Her mother's response was, "That's *probably* true." Chelsea realized her mother would not do that to other people. For example, if Chelsea's husband had said, "It's raining outside," Chelsea's mother would have responded, "Then we'll need umbrellas."

As Chelsea pondered and prayed over this new revelation, God gave her courage to challenge her mother's thinking. The next time her mother answered with "That's probably true," Chelsea very kindly said, "Take the *probably* out of that statement and you've got it right!" Her mother took a quick little breath and said, "That's true."

It's unlikely that Chelsea's mother will change much at this stage in her life, but as Chelsea has allowed God to alter her own perspective, she has become healthier and is beginning to find the real Chelsea.

Remember that our personality types continue to influence us throughout our lives. The elderly Sanguines still want to be stars, get lots of attention, and have people listen and laugh at their stories. Cholerics hate getting old because it means life is slipping out of their control. If possible, put your elderly Choleric parent in charge of something and praise him or her for any minor accomplishment. Melancholy parents may be increasingly depressed and withdrawn. Don't try to jolly them up; just agree with them in their miseries: "Yes, this is a bad day" or "I don't know how you stand the pain!" The older Phlegmatic is usually the easiest to handle if he or she has a TV and is fed. Try to include your Phlegmatic parents in family activities and let them know you value them as persons. They will probably respond.

Doctor God

Dear Florence:

I grew up with a family doctor available for all our questions. He knew our family and the physical weaknesses of each child. At this point I'm in some HMO and I don't even understand what doctor I should go to. It seems that I have to prediagnose my own case and once I've solved the problem, I then find a doctor who specializes in that area. I know I'm exaggerating, but it seems like the truth. If I ask for a second opinion it's as if I'm insulting the doctor. Do I have any rights left at all?

Still Alive in Sacramento

Dear Still Alive:

You and I must have grown up in the same era when women never questioned authority figures. A man of the cloth was considered only one step away from God incarnate. If he uttered a platitude it was as though the burning bush itself had spoken. If a lawyer placed a document before you, you signed. (I sometimes wonder if any of those past ponderous parchments I've autographed without reading will come back to haunt me.) If the doctor told you to take one pill each morning, you took two in hopes you would get better twice as fast. In each situation we were taught to respect the opinion of the professionals and do what we were told. After all, what do we know? We're only women.

When I was a child our family physician was Dr. Sweetsir, and he was spoken of with hushed reverence. I can remember my little grandmother standing in a pious position looking up toward the heavenlies and opening an important sentence with "*Doctor* says . . ." He was never "the doctor" or "Dr. Sweetsir"; he was Doctor. There was an aura of spirituality about the tone of that word, Doctor—putting it on a level with God. Not one of us would have disputed the wisdom that followed. Doctor came when a baby was born or an elder was dying, and whatever he said was what we did.

Doesn't that sound like another world? As you pointed out, our health care today is in such a confused state. We seem to have little choice in doctors. We can hardly find the same doctor twice. When we do, we are impressed with how much more he or she knows than Dr. Sweetsir did and how much equipment he or she has to test us with, but all that knowledge is confined to one part of us. Heart, lungs, eyes, or feet. We have to go to someone else for our other parts. Sometimes modern-day physicians are so busy they make us feel we should have somehow healed ourselves and not bothered them at all. Even though we had another appointment just last week, they often look at us as through a glass darkly, peering quizzically at us, groping for some faint flicker of recognition, which rushes in the minute the nurse hands them our folder full of secrets we can't read from a distance. We make foolish statements in a squeaky voice (caused by the fact that we're freezing because our bare rear is being quick-frozen by the cold steel table). We're embarrassed the gown won't go around us and they're seeing us like this when we wore a perfect little form-fitting ensemble that is now in a wrinkled heap on the chair. Oh, where is Dr. Sweetsir?

Books could be (and have been) written on the medical mistakes perpetrated on women. We could start with the five weeks I spent in one of the country's top hospitals dying of heart attacks, my arm strapped to a board so I could receive blood thinner intravenously, only to find out I wasn't having heart attacks at all. It was my gallbladder that was the problem, but by then my blood was too thin to coagulate for the surgery. Or when I was locked into a huge radioisotope machine and forgotten for four hours until a night watchman came in, woke me up, and asked, "What are you doing here?" As if I'd had a choice!

Most physicians are well informed and caring, but we must remember that we are in charge of our bodies.

Get a Second Opinion

Don't just assume the first doctor you go to is right. If you don't feel right about the diagnosis, get another opinion. Meg got the results of her PAP test and was frightened when they indicated she needed surgery; as a twenty-five-year-old woman she didn't want a hysterectomy. At a friend's suggestion she came to our nutritionist.

Over the years we have seen this talented health-care professional be the instrument for healing in many people who had not received help from regular methods. She set up a program for Meg to follow that she knew from experience would make a difference. The next day Meg called to say that her husband, "a real doctor," wouldn't allow her to continue to see the nutritionist, and because she was under his "headship" she had to do his will. The nutritionist told Meg if she could at least follow the program without coming in to see her she'd counsel her on the phone.

The husband allowed her to take minerals and vitamins though he was sure it was a waste of money. When Meg went for her one-month checkup, the problem had disappeared. Here was a woman who wanted to do the right thing but because of her husband's distorted view of headship might have had unnecessary surgery.

Some of us don't dare question professional opinions; we've bought the lie that we women don't understand our own bodies. Our bodies do communicate warnings if only we listen. *We must study up on our type of ailment.* We should learn the latest information for ourselves; we can't just assume the physician has had time to read *Prevention* magazine. Last year four of my friends found out they had cancer and had been previously misdiagnosed. Let's become knowledgeable before it's too late!

Prevention

We must think preventively and take care of ourselves. Much information is available these days on the dangers of smoking, the need for exercise, and the dangers of food additives and poisons. (Given all the warnings, don't you sometimes wonder if there's anything left you can eat?) We don't need to take nutrition courses to be knowledgeable about our bodies, but none of this information makes any difference if we don't read it and act upon it.

There is much information available on the Internet. The January 11, 1999, issue of *Time Magazine* was dedicated to "The Future of Medicine." As a lay person, I was fascinated to find that life expectancy in the United States jumped from about forty-seven years at the beginning of the century to seventy-six years now. That gives me a few more productive years.

Listen to Your Friends

Dear Florence:

My friend Glenda is a Powerful Choleric high-achiever. She grew up as the eldest of seven with alcoholic parents in a home where she was forced to be the parent of her siblings. She can do twice in a given day what I can do, and I'm no slouch. Her friends and I see Glenda going downhill physically though. We've said to her, "You're killing yourself working like this." Her husband doesn't know what to do and neither do we. What can you do for a Superwoman like Glenda?

Super Friend in South Florida

Dear Super Friend:

What a shame that you can't prevent Glenda from driving herself to the point of destruction. Until she begins to see her folly, she will continue to resist your positive efforts to get help for her. It seems that her place in an alcoholic family led her to make sure no one took advantage of her again or that she would not depend on anyone to meet her needs. She feels she must prove to herself that even though her siblings may not have pulled themselves up, she is going to show them and the world that she can achieve anything she sets out to do. I would talk to her husband again and express your concern. Let him know that you will be available to take her to the doctors when she expresses the need. You obviously see the problems and she is denying them. Robert Burns, the Scottish poet, penned a line which, paraphrased, says, "Wish the gift that God would give us to see ourselves as others see us."

But Glenda didn't listen. She had a driving need to achieve more than anyone else and to perform it all to perfection. She didn't think about her childhood experiences and dysfunctional family; because of her compulsive behavior, she was able to keep herself so busy she didn't have to look at the past. Forced to be parent to her siblings, Glenda learned early to be supermom and supersister combined.

When Glenda married Dan she continued her frenetic pace, leaving him gasping for breath behind her. She had two babies eleven months apart and worked two full-time jobs—one caring for the babies and one as a nurse. As a submissive wife she didn't ask Dan to help. Wasn't she superwoman? People praised her wherever she went.

Glenda worked six nights a week on two hours of sleep a day and became progressively thinner and weaker. It was years before I heard from Glenda herself. Her friends told her they had written to me when they were so worried, and she decided to respond.

Dear Florence:

My good friends, who have always tried to help me, let me know that you were aware of some of my past situation and I decided to update you.

I continued my frantic pace even when my friends warned me of the dangers. I needed to prove myself to me and I became the best in my professional field while adding two more children to our family.

The wake-up call came when I became ill with a rare blood disorder for which there was no cure. Wonder Woman had been struck down. My life had to be prioritized. A dead nurse wasn't going to be much help to four teenagers. My pace slowed somewhat temporarily but the work frenzy flared when I began to feel better, even though I wasn't cured . . . there was no cure.

Later, I was diagnosed with chronic lymphocytic leukemia. Again I prioritized my life and made some changes in work schedules, but as soon as I began to feel better the pace resumed.

Now, two rounds of chemotherapy later and after some serious introspection, God, yes God, has convicted me that I must do the emotional work that has been so pitifully neglected and begin to deal with the cause of my compulsive behavior. Last August, when I was unable to speak after having a stroke in a grocery store parking lot, I knew I must address my self-destructive behaviors and stop asking my physical body to bear the brunt of unresolved emotional pain. Through counseling I have begun to face, experience, and resolve my very deep emotional wounds by taking God back into those places and discovering His incredible loving hand. Unexpectedly and very gratefully, my cancer is in remission and I am healthier than I have been in ten years. My oncologist is amazed and believes me when I say I am better . . . spiritually, emotionally, and physically, as my blood count confirms.

How I wish I had listened to my very wise friends years ago. Maybe I wouldn't have cancer and wonder at my future. Thank you for caring. Tell other women to listen to their friends who have their best interests at heart. Don't try to be a superwoman like I did. Take control of your life in a positive, healthy way. I learned that lesson too late.

Grateful Glenda

Dear Glenda:

Thanks for sharing your first-hand experience. You're right, women need to learn to take control of their lives before it's too late. If the people who care the most for you are warning that your behaviors are destructive, have the courage to investigate your motives and begin the healing process before it costs you your health or your life.

Some of us are so preoccupied with our jobs and caring for our families that we neglect ourselves, as Glenda did. Some feel it's better not to know. "What you don't know won't hurt you." But in fact, what you don't know can kill you.

According to the National Breast Cancer Coalition there are 2.6 million women in this country with breast cancer, but one million of them don't know it yet and may not until it's too late.[1]

Mammograms and self-examinations are considered essential along with regular medical checkups. When it's time for your mammogram it is wise to go to a clinic accredited by the American College of Radiology. To check this, call the National Cancer Institute's information line, 800–4-CANCER, for the name of a certified lab near you.

We as women can no longer afford to neglect our own health and expect to live the abundant life we are promised. If we are being taken advantage of by our children, parents, relatives, guests, partners, or our own superwoman complex, we need to stop, look, and listen. We must take control of our lives.

Dealing with Divorce and Widowhood

Dear Florence:

In my Bible study I have several divorced women. The others don't associate much with them and one even asked me why I let "sinners" into the group. Why can't Christians accept others, no matter what they've been through?

Open Minded in Ontario

Dear Open Minded:

The majority of Christian women I see each day who are going through divorces didn't want them. The majority never even thought it was a possibility and were totally unprepared to deal with the stark reality when it hit them. In many cases the traditional advice they received from their church leaders was to be submissive, hang in there, and pray more. Because they were ashamed to tell anyone and often did not have the money to get legal counsel, many have ended up broke, on welfare, living in substandard housing, and leaving children uncared for while they try to earn a living.

163

We would all like to look the other way and utter platitudes about trusting the Lord, but we can't play ostrich anymore. We must wake up to the fact that good, dedicated, Christian women are in financial and emotional trouble because of divorce. We can no longer treat them as fallen women—as so many report they are made to feel—but to help them face the harsh reality of life as a single woman. Of the divorced women I talk with, none are out nights carousing in singles bars. Instead they are home helping with homework and doing housework after a long day with low pay. And they're trying to convince their children that the Christian life is exciting.

We should not view divorce as a simple alternative to marriage problems, nor should we condemn those going through it. We need to help others touch base with reality and help the church, Bible study teachers, and counselors to accept victims with compassion. As leaders we must be aware of the pitfalls of divorce proceedings and show women how to get proper advice. As people untutored in divorce law we cannot possibly make judgments on the proceedings, but we should know someone, preferably in the church body, who can help.

Without kindness and affirmation from the church, divorce victims may decide to leave the church. In your group have each woman introduce herself and give her personal needs for prayer. This should shift the attitude from condemnation to compassion.

The Faults of No-Fault Divorce

Dear Florence:

My sister is going through a divorce and she is so emotionally exhausted she doesn't seem to be making sensible decisions. She throws around terms like "no fault" and "equitable distribution" but she has no idea what it's all about. Could you walk me through what she needs to do? Please show me the pitfalls.

Pretending in Pittsburgh

Dear Pretending:

Let's pretend that you have been served divorce papers and are in a state of shock. You are trying to wake up and you need some help. We hope you have copies of expenses and records of all financial dealings. You'll be glad you did if, in a few days, you discover your departing husband has taken all the papers and put them in his lawyer's hand before he sues you for divorce. Unfortunately, hiding papers with a lawyer is an increasingly common practice that makes it impossible for a wife to prove anything. If you have copies of records of real estate deeds, properties, insurance, etc., you will be better prepared to fight for what you deserve. It costs money to have a lawyer search out hidden or misplaced documents. Don't automatically take your suing husband's word that you don't need a lawyer. He may tell you that his lawyer, a fine and fair man, will take care of you both and will save you money. Not usually true. There may be exceptions, but in general his lawyer is interested only in him. You need someone on your side. I have seen some lovely Christian women who didn't get legal help and who ended up with nothing.

In the past spouses seeking divorce had to prove adultery or extreme mental cruelty. People worked overtime to find evidence to be used against each other, even staging what appeared to be adultery—with photographers handy. On January 1, 1970, California was the first state to institute no-fault divorce, meaning spouses no longer had to find something scandalous about their mates to get divorced. Irreconcilable differences became the new measure of divorce, and those differences could be stretched to fit around almost anything.

When no-fault divorce was initiated, it was supposed to ease the agony of court hearings and dignify the process of dissolving a marriage. But it hasn't worked that way. A *Woman's Day* article on no-fault divorce said:

> Instead of becoming simpler, divorce legislation has multiplied into a tangle of laws and regulations that even divorce lawyers cannot always find their way through. No two states have the same laws, and so many statutes are under scrutiny in the courts that interpretations change from one month to the next.
>
> Most disappointing of all, the changes in divorce laws have let down women in their expectation of better financial treatment.

165

Perhaps such a hope never was realistic—when an ordinary family's financial pie is cut in two, neither half is very large. Often there is just not enough money to go around. But today, as in the past, most women still come out poorly, even when the laws dictate what looks like a reasonable split.[1]

By mutual consent a couple could get divorced and, with any luck, receive what is called "equitable distribution" of their properties and assets. *Equitable,* of course, depended on the judge or mediator making the decisions. If this person was a man who had just been taken to the cleaners by his wife, he probably wouldn't be inclined to favor you! This is where your records of all major purchases become valuable.

Another term that has developed is "spousal contribution." If you put your husband through medical school or worked to build his business, you could be entitled to some recompense in the settlement. However, you will need documentation of what you have done. A wife named Josie learned that the hard way. She helped in her husband's car business, working for no salary for ten years. When he divorced her and she tried to get "spousal contribution" she could show no records of the hours she had worked and it wasn't allowed.

With these new divorce laws, which were intended to give women equal distribution of property, came some losses. In the past most divorced women got alimony and child support to some degree, but in today's system only 15 percent of the women going through divorces get any alimony. There are four kinds of alimony: *permanent, lump sum, remunerative* (for the wife who put money into the marriage or put the husband through school), and *rehabilitative* (designed to help you learn a skill so you can support yourself). If you look too intelligent and competent you may not win rehabilitative alimony. In fact, if you look strong enough to bus tables at McDonald's you may be perceived as skilled enough to support yourself and the little ones without further training.

Women, in general, earn 71 percent of what men earn for comparable work and on the executive level only 42 percent of what men receive. So the financial outlook for a divorced woman rearing children is not optimistic. Most women, like your sister, settle for too little too quickly in order to stop the pain of the divorce proceedings; many women get small awards because they have no records. A lawyer will help you, but he can't produce your records. I hope this information will allow you to help your sister through the divorce process with understanding.

Don't Let Yourself Be a Victim

Dear Florence:

I need a quick course on how to handle divorce. I'm hopeful my husband will change his mind, but at the moment he has moved out and threatened to take me for all I'm worth. I'm not really worth much, but I need some advice. Do I just give him everything or what? It might be much easier.

Worthless in Winona

Dear Worthless:

Please stop looking at yourself as worthless. Just that attitude will make you seem the victim. Avoiding conflict will only hurt you in the long run. In looking for an example of a woman who handled the divorce procedure as positively as possible, I called my friend Sheila, a Christian writer. I had known her before, during, and after her divorce, and I felt she would have some encouraging words for women facing these difficult times. When she wrote me, I felt what she said was so well crafted that I'm quoting her directly:

One of my first concerns was credit because Les, my ex-husband, had canceled my name on all our credit cards without warning. Fortunately, I did have a Master Card in my own name that had been offered to me at some time prior to the separation. I had forgotten I even had it and am not sure why I did, but it turned out to be my salvation. Also, of all the other cards, JCPenney contacted me and offered me a card in my name based on a good past credit history. If a woman contacts the companies where she and her husband have had joint credit, she can explain the situation and at least some of them will issue her credit in her own name. As it turned out, because I had the one major credit card in my name I had no problem establishing my own credit. I used it to set up several credit accounts and used them a little so I could begin to establish my own credit history. As a result I was able to buy a home in my name (two years later) based on that credit history.

Shortly after we separated, my husband's accountant invited me to lunch to offer me what amounted to a divorce settlement. He tried to convince me that Les's business was in serious trouble (so it was not worth very much), but Les was willing to take the business and give me the house (valued then at $250,000). He tried to assure me that this was a good deal for me. Les was hoping I would agree to this settlement and he wouldn't have to get a lawyer. I turned it down because I didn't want to keep the house (I had already moved out), I wasn't sure if it would sell or for how much, and I didn't have the resources to maintain it in the meantime. I also was not ready to file for divorce and didn't want to be pushed into something before I was ready. As it turned out, that was a wise decision.

Next, I found a book on legal issues for women. It explained that if I settled for alimony, I would have to pay taxes on the monthly payments, but if I took a property settlement, I did not have to pay taxes on the principle (just the interest). As it turned out, I did get a property settlement that amounted to monthly payments for several years. When the house sold I was to get a lump-sum payment of half of whatever he got as a cash down payment up to a maximum of thirty thousand dollars, which would offset part of what he was to pay me in the property settlement. He tried to sell the house and each time he got a potential buyer, he tried to get me to carry the loan so he could get out from under it, but I refused each time. Even though I would have made more money on the interest, etc., and he tried to assure me I could resell the house and make even more if the buyers defaulted, my main concern was the expense of maintaining the house and grounds if there had been a problem. As it turned out, he decided to keep the house and is still living there, so I continue to get monthly payments on the property settlement. Fortunately, he has always kept up-to-date on the payments. So collecting payments for what will be a total of eleven years hasn't been a problem. However, if a woman has serious concerns about her husband skipping out or not making the monthly payments, this might not be the wisest option. The other advantage of having the property settlement is that it is counted as a tangible asset by banks, etc.

At one point I had to meet with Les and the lawyers so they could take a deposition on our assets (to make sure neither of us was hiding any assets the other didn't know about). Prior to that meeting, I did my homework and went into the meeting knowing everything I needed to know to answer their questions. I had moved out of the big house into an apartment so I made up a list of what furnishings I had taken with me, which ones Les had, what I'd given to the children, etc., along with the estimated value of each piece. Since I was not getting any support from him at that time and was asking for it, I had a detailed copy of my budget and projected income. Les came to the meeting with no notes and could only guess when asked a question. I was so well prepared that even though his lawyer did his best to rattle me he wasn't able to ask a single question I wasn't prepared to answer. As a result I got the financial support I asked for, and his lawyer found out I couldn't be intimated into doing what they wanted.

I let my lawyer know up front that I only wanted my fair share and I wasn't interested in taking Les for everything I could get, and he honored that; but he always let me know how to best handle the requests or what was fair. For example, Les had taken my car away several months before we separated because he wanted me to be forced to ask to borrow his car so he'd always know where I was. I contended that I should have my own car as I had for years, so eventually I got back the car without paying for it.

My advice to other women is to not let yourself become a victim or to play the role of a victim. I realize that in some cases they don't have a choice, but I know there are also a lot of women who become victims simply because they don't find out their rights and stand up for them. There is no excuse for a woman not knowing about the family assets, etc., and knowing how to handle the family finances. In my case, being well prepared and informed at each juncture is what helped me come out as well as I did. I would not let them intimidate me into doing what they wanted if it was not advantageous to me as well. I found it best never to give an answer on the spot, but to wait until I could think it through logically and unemotionally.

I went for counseling and felt it was important to get myself to a place where I felt well and whole again before I got into the really emotional garbage of actually getting the divorce. It was about eighteen months after the separation that the divorce went through. I am grateful I was able to take it slowly. Don't ever rush into a divorce.

How fortunate that Sheila had done her homework and had the stamina to hang in there until a fair settlement was reached. She is a role model for other women going through this ordeal.

Custody and Visitation Issues

Dear Florence:

My ex-husband and I got through the financial part of our divorce okay, but we still argue about who should have the children most of the time. Our lawyers advised that the kids live with me and suggested we have a general agreement that provides for "reasonable visitation" for my ex-husband. At first things went okay, but now he sometimes doesn't show on time to get them, or he'll be late in bringing them back. I worry terribly and it makes me angry that he won't respect the schedule I give him. Doesn't he have to follow the schedule I set since I have custody of the children? To make matters worse, he just announced he is engaged and after he is married he is going to try to seek custody of the children because they will have a two-parent home! Can he do that? Those are my kids and she is not their mother! Don't the courts rule that children should be with their mother?

Scared in Scottsdale

Dear Scared:

There's just no telling today what the courts will and will not rule in the case of families of divorce. It's good that you and your ex-husband were able to work out the financial part of your divorce, but as you have learned there are many more important issues to deal with. You are right to be concerned about custody of the children, and it is all the more reason to retain a lawyer who not only specializes in family law but who is familiar with the judges and mediators in your district. Do you remember the story of Vera, who decided to flee from her abusive husband for the safety of her life, assumed her son would be safe temporarily, and left him home? Her husband filed charges of abandonment, and she has not seen her son since that time. Mothers are not always guaranteed custody of their children.

While our court system was set up to be fair and impartial, it is often subject to the emotional whims of whoever is sitting on the bench on a given day. If your husband is not honoring your schedule with the children and you may be facing custody issues, you will need to educate yourself about your legal parenting, custody, and his visitation right. And take the necessary steps to protect those rights.

In her book *How to Be First in a Second Marriage* Rose Sweet gives a detailed and practical checklist to help divorced parents set up a schedule to benefit both parents and children. Rose advises that in a divorce, there are always new *roles, rights,* and *responsibilities* for parents. One of the women she counseled had written to her, "I thought we could get along after the divorce and we could work out visitation. I didn't want to be petty about specific dates and times. As soon as the first Christmas came we fought about where the children should spend Christmas Day. My ex didn't bring the kids home on time and we ended up with a cold Christmas dinner. It was the worst holiday ever and the children were in tears. I learned the value of a specific visitation order which can be enforced by the courts, spelling out dates and times for both parties. Having a clear visitation agreement is not mean or spiteful, it's smart!"[2] The book also covers some of the emotional, financial, and legal issues that women will have to deal with if their husbands remarry. Instead of living in fear about what will happen with our divorced spouses in the future, we should keep ourselves prepared and protected.

Surviving Widowhood

Dear Florence:

I am getting on in years and wondering how important it is that my husband and I have wills. We have a good marriage and loving children who would handle everything in a positive way. Legally, do I have to have one? What would happen if I didn't?

Will-less in Williamsburg

Dear Will-less:

There are no will police who will come into your home and force you to make a will, but without one you leave your survivors with trouble they don't need and the government with the ability to eat up what you thought was secure. Either call a lawyer to set up a simple will or buy a kit with instructions and papers to do it yourself. Let me give you two samples of survivors with no will to turn to.

Kathryn seemed to have it all. She was married to a doctor, had a big house and fancy cars, plenty of money, and no need to work. Her husband loved her and the children and wanted them to have what he'd been deprived of as a child. Kathryn wrote about her experience:

> I was married to a general surgeon whose temperament was super Choleric. He wanted to control and take care of his family in the way he had dreamed of as a child but never had a chance to live. His desire was to let me just have fun and take care of the four kids as they grew up—and *eventually,* he said, he would teach me about money. I was Sanguine enough to say, "Great! That's easy enough!" So I let it happen and I knew nothing about his finances.
>
> But one day my bubble burst. He died suddenly of a massive coronary. I had to grow up fast and close his office, refer patients, take care of all the business and funeral arrangements, *before* I could even *grieve.* My husband never wanted to admit he was mortal, so he never wrote a will or taught me the ropes. I had to become Choleric (which I was underneath, but didn't realize). Now I really like my personality, but it was hell getting there.
>
> Tell other women to learn about their husband's business, finances, and will. If he doesn't have one—because he doesn't expect to die—suggest that you go together. Then *make the appointment.* Ignorance is *not* bliss.

Shelley's story was different than Kathryn's. She had worked side by side with her counselor husband for many years, handling all the bookkeeping for his practice. Eventually their son joined the firm as a counselor also and her husband taught him all he knew.

When Shelley's husband died suddenly, she didn't know who owned what. They'd never discussed this possibility. She had a simple will in her hand that stated the proceeds of the practice were to be divided equally between Shelley and her son James. James asked if he could make monthly payments to her out of the profits of the practice as he did not have enough money to give her a cash settlement. Since she was doing the books and could keep tabs on the financial condition of the business, Shelly felt comfortable with this agreement. After all, she was his mother.

But soon after her husband's death, James hired a part-time bookkeeper under the guise of "giving Mom some free time." Shelley didn't really feel she needed any free time, but the leadership of her church told her she should comply with her son's requests and let him be her leader. She was under his umbrella, they said. After a few months James had cut Shelley's hours completely, and the part-time bookkeeper had become full-time. One day when Shelley stopped by the office, she noticed there was new furniture and each room had been completely redecorated. Then she found out James had borrowed money against the business, which he claimed was to pay for the redecorating.

Eventually the monthly payments to Shelley stopped. When she inquired, he told her that business was slow, he had a lot of debts, and she would have to wait for her money. That's when Shelley came to me. When I suggested she contact a lawyer immediately, she asked, "As a Christian, is that all right for me to do?" Shelley's husband thought he had provided for her, but he didn't take into account that his son might become greedy. Shelley needed someone to give her permission to stand up for her legal portion of her husband's business. Of course, the problem was compounded because the person who was cheating her was her son.

Widows have to make many decisions very quickly and, as we have cited here, often times they are completely unprepared to become the sole decision-maker in their family.

The American Association of Retired Persons (AARP) has published a book entitled *Survival Handbook for Widows*. It provides **173** this helpful list of ways to protect yourself against those who would like to help you spend your deceased husband's money.

1. Learn to say no.
2. Deal with responsible, reliable local dealers or services.
3. Never buy on a door-to-door salesperson's first trip to your home.
4. Don't be afraid to ask what you may think the other person will think are dumb questions. They are cheaper than dumb mistakes.
5. Never buy sight unseen.
6. Read and understand contracts before signing.
7. Check with someone who knows the product before you buy, not after.
8. Stay within your income. Do not be oversold.

Suspect a phony if any of the following apply:

1. You are asked to sign your name—now.
2. The prices are too good to be true.
3. The salesperson discredits others who sell similar products.
4. A cash payment is necessary.
5. The contract has vague or tricky wording.[3]

Actually such suggestions also apply to those of us who are divorced or single. We tend to expect the best of others and can easily be taken in by a smooth salesman preying on vulnerable women.

Remember, if it seems too good to be true, it probably is!

Dating Again

Dear Florence:

My name is Lyndsay. I was married with three children when my twenty-four-year-old husband was diagnosed with cancer. He died a short time later. Convinced that my children needed a dad and I needed a husband to take care of me financially, I began dating and frantically searching. I encouraged all of my friends and relatives to play matchmaker and I wasn't discriminating or particular on the qualifications. Eight months to the day after my husband's death, I married a man I hardly knew, but he looked good, said the right words, and went to church each Sunday. In fact, I met him in church.

My emotional needs and the fear for my children's future led me to make a tragic choice. My new husband developed incestuous relationships with both of my daughters and left me for another new divorcée.

I have had to pay a great price for what I hoped would be financial and emotional security, and so have my children.

Learned Too Late

When I later asked Lyndsay what her advice would be for other widows or divorcées facing a newly single life, she gave me this list:

1. Grieving takes time; don't panic!
2. Know who *you* are so you can discern who *he* is. Study the Personalities.
3. Don't allow others to be matchmakers—*you* have to live with the person you marry!
4. God can meet all your needs in *his* time—financial, emotional, and security—and he can even fill your heart where it is empty. I've learned that.
5. Don't rush—take your time! Know all you can about him first.

Soon after I talked with Lyndsay, I met with a group of women who had been divorced and remarried. As we relaxed together after a seminar, I asked them what advice they would give someone heading into a second marriage. They all said in unison: "Do a credit check on him." "Do a Dunn and Bradstreet." "Look at his credit report." They all laughed at the similarity of their answers and then told me their stories.

Each of them had met a man who was attractive, well-dressed, successful, and sensitive. Ironically, all of them had met these men at Christian singles groups and they had eventually prayed together about getting married. The other similarity was that the men had **175** all been deceptive about money. Even though they weren't exactly Christian con men, they had not told the truth.

One man had lied to his wife-to-be that he had a job when he didn't. In fact, he still had not gone to work even after they had been married quite a while; she had ended up supporting him. One woman found out after the marriage that her new husband owed sixty thousand dollars in back taxes and was in trouble with the IRS. One man had a very close relationship with his secretary, who paid the couple's bills and refused to give the new wife any money without a written request. Each of these women felt betrayed and knew they could never totally trust the person they had pledged to live with forever. When we got beyond their case histories and back to their advice, they all had plenty to say based on their experiences. Here's a summary of their suggestions:

1. *Check his finances.* Even though it sounds unromantic, the time to discuss finances is *before* the wedding, not after. If you are considering marriage, you should each get your own TRW (or similar) report, then sit down without stress and share them with each other. Sometimes you will be surprised at what information TRW has on you. Fred and I recently found we had a negative rating on something our son had not handled correctly and it had mistakenly been put on Fred's account. When you both expose your ratings before marriage, there are no ugly surprises later on. Make sure you both have your finances in order before you marry.

2. *Discuss how you will handle your monthly expenses.* You need to agree ahead of time who will pay for what. Are there child-support obligations from a first marriage? Ask. Don't wait for surprises. Who will handle taxes, rent, car payments? Don't be afraid to ask questions. If he turns you down because you want to discuss finances, you know he has something to hide or he is a very insecure man and you don't need him.

In the book *Love and the Law* author Gail Koff considers it mandatory for those going into second or third marriages to have a prenuptial agreement. These are relatively simple legal preparations that spell out finances, ownership, and responsibilities and, according to

Koff's experience, are more than worth their weight in gold. Prenuptial agreements serve two major purposes: They get emotional issues over money settled when you're both positive, and they set at ease the concerns of both families. Prenups, as they are called, supersede state laws and will save future grief. Don't fall for the line, "If you really loved me you wouldn't ask these things. Just trust me."

3. *Check pensions, wills, and insurance policies.* Don't wait until you are married to find out that all his insurance goes to his first wife, that his pension fund is in her name, and that the sole beneficiaries of his will are his children. He has a right to do with these policies as he will, but you should understand ahead of time. I frequently hear women say, "If I'd only known, I wouldn't have married him." Once you have discussed these issues you can record the details of the agreement in your prenups.

4. *Meet with his first wife.* If you're considering marriage to a man who has been married before, see if his first wife will talk with you, or meet with one of her good friends. (Of course if you were "the other woman" in the divorce, this would not be advisable.) Although the perspective you get may be weighted against your prospective husband, the information may save you from a costly mistake. Ask why the marriage failed and what he should have done differently. One woman found out from the first wife that her fiancé was homosexual and was marrying her as a cover. Another learned her intended husband was so attached to his mother that she controlled his every move. Still another found out the man was a compulsive liar and had abused his daughter. It is not rude of you to learn all you can about a man who is going to live with you and your own children. Save yourself surprises. In 1989 in Massachusetts a survey done by the legal profession showed that only 35 percent of the financial statements submitted by men were accurate. Are you going to be fortunate enough to find an honest man out of that 35 percent?

5. *Don't give up who you really are.* Don't be afraid to be yourself just so you will please him. Fear will always destroy you. It will transform you into a nonperson and he won't like you any better.

6. *Don't rush into anything just to be married.* Be willing to pay the price for the knowledge you need to make a wise decision. **177**

7. *Date someone for at least a full year before jumping into a new marriage.* By dating for a year you will experience holidays, birthdays, Mother's Day, and any anniversaries together, giving you the opportunity to observe him and his reactions to different situations. Also observe how his family relates on holidays, what expectations they have, and where his children from his first marriage fit into the picture. Make sure he has dealt with the emotional ties to his first wife and is not still bound to her by unresolved guilt, fear, or bitterness.

8. *Find out what his priorities are and where you will fit in.* Does he put his job, mother, hobbies, ex-wife, or children before you? Will you be first or last in a second marriage?

9. *Find out if he is open to growth and change.* Is he willing to take the time to learn about you and how to meet your emotional needs? Have you put your own needs aside during the courtship so that you don't have to deal with any potential difficulties?

10. *Listen to your close and trusted friends.* Be more open to their opinions, concerns, and advice. So often the adage "love is blind" is so true. Knowing that should make us even more cautious.

One of the women I spoke with concluded, "If I had it to do over again I would stay true to my own Sanguine personality. I would look inside myself to find my own emotional needs. I would get to know and understand myself instead of getting caught up in the excitement of being in love and living the happily-ever-after syndrome."

She then summed up her experience this way: "I realize I wore a Phlegmatic mask, pretending to be sweetly submissive, and it just about killed me, physically and emotionally." Remember, as Shakespeare said, "This above all: to thine own self be true."

Don't Be Blinded by Your Neediness

Dear Florence:

I've been a single mom for about six months now and I'm not sure how much longer I can take this pressure. My ex-husband doesn't give us much support, and I don't think my paycheck will be able to keep covering the bill's each month. It's hard to have to make all the decisions on my own when I know my children are counting on me to take care of them. I just wish I could meet a nice Christian man to take care of all of us. Maybe I should start going to our church's singles class. What do you think?

Anxious in Aberdene

Dear Anxious:

I know you're feeling an overwhelming amount of pressure right now, but don't let your emotional and financial needs push you into a new relationship. Too many singles are so focused on looking for someone to be with that they can't see anything else.

"Sometimes I think this Sunday school class is a Christian singles bar." These were the words of the singles pastor of a large church where I was about to speak. "They come in here with one thought on their minds, and I'm helpless to do anything about it."

This pastor was doing his best to teach God's principles to adult singles, but he shrugged his shoulders in a gesture of hopelessness. "At least the ones they pick up are Christians, so I guess that's better than going to the bars." By the time he'd shared his frustrations with me, we'd arrived on the platform and I was facing a bright, attractive group of singles who were all singing their hearts out.

After the service the pastor turned me over to Lucy, who was assigned to take me out to lunch. "She's the most faithful of all and will do anything to help," he said as he introduced her. Off we went to lunch, where Lucy told me her story. I asked if I could take notes so her experiences could help someone else. "If you can save one woman from going through what I've experienced, feel free!" she said.

Lucy had met Jeff at this church. Both had been divorced three years and had children the same ages. Tall, dark, and good-looking, Jeff was deeply involved with the ministry . . . making pancakes on Sundays, inviting single parents over for potlucks at his house, leading singles events. He was the obvious catch of the group.

As Lucy gravitated into a leadership position, their contact was more frequent and a friendship began to bloom. After a few months the singles director of their division asked them to teach a class **179** together on "How to Have a Healthy Relationship." Since neither one had ever had one of those, both were intrigued. They met and began working on approaches to take. By the end of their second meeting, it was obvious that they were attracted to each other. He was perfect. A strong Christian, a devoted single dad. She, too, loved the Lord and was dedicated to his service and to her children. Both loved to hike, body surf, cook, and travel. It was truly a match made in heaven.

After the third date, Lucy sensed he was about to kiss her. She said, "I hadn't been touched in a loving way for so long . . . I was ready. But the kiss was rough. He shoved me into the kitchen counter and began tearing at my clothes, going for it. I said, 'No.' He didn't stop, but he did become more gentle. The next day he called me, full of remorse, and bemoaned the way his 'flesh' had gotten the better of him.

"Red flag!" Lucy said, waving her arm. "I saw it in my peripheral vision, but I'd been alone for what felt like forever. So I ignored it. Mistake."

They were practically inseparable after that. Their children bonded. Jeff's daughter called Lucy Mommy. They became, in the singles director's words, the shining stars of her ministry, planning and running events ranging from a single-parents camping trip to Mother's Day and Father's Day parties.

A few months later Jeff's daughter had a birthday. Who showed up uninvited to the party? Jeff's former girlfriend, Danielle. Everywhere they went for the next week or so, Danielle managed to be there. Jeff assured Lucy that they were merely talking through some old issues, that it was no big deal. She did her best to be pleasant, but underneath felt a perplexing, overwhelming sense of impending doom.

"I'd wake up in the middle of the night in a panic . . . wondering, wondering, wondering. Then Danielle called me one morning and informed me that she'd had sex with Jeff four times since that birthday party. I hung up on her. She called again and threatened to go to the church with her story and destroy him. I hung up and called Jeff."

Lucy continued, getting more angry as she relived these moments. "He began to cry and beg for forgiveness, saying that Danielle had manipulated him into bed and that he loved me, only me. He kept calling her the 'ex-girlfriend from hell.'"

Lucy forgave him. They went to the singles director and shared their story with her, and Jeff asked for forgiveness there too. Danielle also repented. Restoration was achieved in the Christian way. Lucy even hugged Danielle one Sunday after church and offered her forgiveness.

All seemed to be back to normal until three weeks later, when Jeff confessed that he'd spent the evening with Danielle.

She told him, "I'm not into triangles. I didn't sign up for this ride! Either you quit seeing her or you have to stop seeing me!"

Jeff flipped. His whole personality changed when he felt threatened. He called Lucy a "controlling bitch" who wanted to put him in a little box, make him her prisoner. Suddenly, Lucy was the evil one, Danielle the angel.

In her pain, Lucy asked the singles director to excuse her from being in leadership at the next few events. She attended, however, and to her chagrin, Danielle and Jeff were up front, being publicly commended for their hard work. She had taken Lucy's man and her place in the ministry. What was going on here?

Lucy recounted, "Every time I went to the church after that, at least one of my children would leave in tears. Hysterical, awful tears. Not only was I out, but my kids were being rejected and humiliated too. I went to the singles director, but my pleas for intervention fell on deaf ears.

"When should I have awakened?" Lucy asked me. "After he practically raped me on the kitchen counter? If not at that point, then how about after Danielle's phone calls? I could have saved myself and my kids immeasurable heartache.

"But no, I was so desperate to be loved that I ignored the warning signals, and there certainly were enough of them! I fell for a self-sacrificing, religious man who appeared to be the perfect daddy. I believed his words of love, family, and forever. I gave myself to him sexually even after I knew he'd cheated on me." Lucy burst into tears.

What can we learn from Lucy's unfortunate experience?

There are two issues to ponder here. The first is that we can't be blinded by a man's apparent piety. All of us must walk our talk.

Single women . . . you may be lonely and longing for love, but do not let your judgment be blinded by neediness! By succumbing to Jeff's sexual advances and believing his promises, Lucy became intimately involved with him before she had a clear idea of his character. And his goodness was counterfeit.

God instructs us to refrain from sexual activity until marriage. His reasons for this are to protect us from wounding ourselves and each other and to prevent us from contracting serious disease. And in the case of single parents, God wants to protect the children from being wounded as well.

Single women . . . so many of you came of age in the sixties and seventies. You left the churches of your youth and became part of the sexual revolution. Although you probably remained faithful in your marriages, if you once again face single life, your sexual behavior may revert back to that of the seventies. Even though you're a Christian now, you're still looking for love in physical relationships. In your yearning for connection and affection, you may bypass the vital steps of verifying the other's integrity or investigating their sexual history—blood tests are a vital part of premarital precautions today.

Sadly, not all pious men are true! It is possible to be deceived and used as Lucy was. If this story sounds familiar . . . if you're involved with or are contemplating involvement with someone in your church . . . slow down! He may be using religion as a facade, a tool for seduction. Find out how many others he's dated in the group and for how long.

There is a hopeful ending to Lucy's story. Her church did not abandon her. She wrote a letter to her pastor, the one I had met, and he responded in love and wisdom. Jeff and Danielle were exposed and removed from the singles ministry. The singles director was replaced by a healthy married couple . . . a couple who had been through divorce, been down in the trenches, who had suffered and made mistakes comparable to those of the people they were ministering to. Their compassion and true Christian maturity have been a gift to the singles ministry of their church as they have taken their troubles and turned them into a blessing for others. As Paul wrote to the Corinthian believers, "The God of all comfort . . . comforts us in all our troubles, so that we can comfort those in any trouble with the comfort we ourselves have received from God" (2 Cor. 1:3–4 NIV).

ten

I'll Pray about It

All good Christian women believe in prayer. How frightening it would be to think there was no one up there to call on in time of need! Yet some of us have a cloudy view of a God afar off and a Jesus who is somehow untouchable. When we hear of someone who has a "prayer life," we feel guilty over our "prayer minute." When there's a prayer meeting at church with no refreshments, we rush to the mall instead for some urgent item. When we tell a friend, "I'll pray about it," we forget.

Oswald Chambers wrote: "Never *say* you will pray about a thing; *pray about it.* Our Lord's teaching about prayer is so amazingly simple but at the same time so amazingly profound that we are apt to miss His meaning. The danger is to water down what Jesus says about prayer and make it mean something more like common sense; if it were only common sense, it was not worth His while to say it."[1]

Does Prayer Really Work?

Dear Florence:
    Recently I went to our church counselor about a problem with my children. The counselor told me my problem wasn't the children, but

that I didn't pray enough. He made me feel like I wasn't spiritual enough. As I've thought about it, I think he's right. I don't really pray at all, I just send up quick requests in times of need. Am I the only Christian with prayer problems?

Prayerless in Pasadena

Dear Prayerless:

You are not alone. Many believe Christians want to pray, and they feel guilty when they don't. Many like you limit themselves to what I call "emergency prayer"—calling to God when all else fails. We take control of our lives in many ways, but often we don't do well with prayer. Don't waste time feeling guilty; instead, start praying.

How do you develop a prayer life? How do you get to know Jesus? The best way Fred and I have found is to write your prayers. Try writing a letter to Jesus. When we teach this simple technique in seminars, we instruct people to write a simple letter to Jesus every day. This isn't a letter for anyone else to read, so it doesn't have to be perfect. You can share your problems with Jesus without fear of harsh judgment—he won't berate you for not being spiritual enough. As you pour out your feelings to Jesus, you will begin to get to know him in a personal way. Instead of a far off God, Jesus will be your counselor and friend.

We have received many testimonies of changed lives when people start to pray sincerely. Writing forces us to concentrate on what we're doing instead of allowing our minds to wander to our grocery lists or the TV schedule. Writing to Jesus makes us think about him as a real person who cares about us. Writing keeps us accountable each day. Either we wrote in our notebook or we didn't. We can't just sort of pray as we weave through traffic.

We also teach "listening prayer" by encouraging the participants to write out a question to the Lord and then record everything that comes to their minds. We give them quiet time to do this. As we ask them to share, we are amazed at what God has said to individuals, giving custom-tailored answers that affirm the power of God. Many have said, "That's the first time I knew that Jesus could answer my prayers."

Achieving Two-Way Communication with God

Dear Florence:

I heard you speak about writing your prayers, but when I sit down to do this, no words seem to come to me. Do you have some steps or outlines I could use to get me started?

No-Words in Nebraska

Dear No-Words:

Many people experience difficulty with writing their prayers. When we first begin, writing to Jesus seems presumptuous and sometimes even frightening. Does he hear? Does he care? Will he answer?

One of the best outlines I've know was written by Marilyn Heavilin when she was on our CLASS staff. When she presents this lesson, she gives the audience time to do each step on paper. This gives people a jump start on writing to Jesus. Marilyn calls this plan "two-way communication."[2] Use this for your outline and then teach it to your family, Sunday school class, or friends. If you can help one or two others to pray as well, you will be thrilled with the results.

1. *Affection.* Many times because of damage in our childhood, the hardest words for us to receive from the Lord are, "I love you." Listen quietly. If the first words you hear are the words of condemnation, write them down in your notebook, and then write across those words, "These words are a lie! Romans 8:1 states, 'There is therefore now no condemnation to them which are in Christ Jesus, who walk not after the flesh, but after the Spirit.'"

Keep listening until you hear that still, small voice whisper, "I love you!" Then write it down and thank Jesus for his everlasting love.

2. *Reflection.* Often we get in the middle of a mess and we think, *How in the world will I ever get out of this?* In Deuteronomy 5:6 the Lord states, in essence, "Remember that you were slaves in Egypt and that the Lord your God brought you out of there with a mighty hand and an outstretched arm."

187

Take time to reflect on the Egypts God has brought you out of and write them down. Thank God for rescuing you then, and thank him for how he is going to rescue you this time. Write down the thoughts he gives you.

3. *Correction.* First we need to examine ourselves to see if there is something we need to confess, someone we need to forgive, or someone we need to ask to forgive us. Also, this is a time when we can ask God if he wants to change our perspective on something. This could be a current situation or something that happened to us in our childhood. As God brings a memory to our minds, we can invite him into the scene and ask him to give us his perspective. In your prayer time, write down what the Lord shows you. "Behold, thou desirest truth in the inward parts: and in the hidden part thou shalt make me to know wisdom" (Ps. 51:6).

4. *Direction.* "I will instruct thee and teach thee in the way which thou shalt go: I will guide thee with mine eye" (Ps. 32:8). As we learn to ask the Lord specific questions, he will give us specific answers. "Your teachers will be hidden no more; with your own eyes you will see them. Whether you turn to the right or to the left, your ears will hear a voice behind you, saying, 'This is the way; walk in it'" (Isa. 30:20–21 NIV).

5. *Inspection.* We must always compare what we hear with Scripture. Scripture is the final and true authority for the Christian, so if what we hear contradicts Scripture, we should ignore what we hear and hang on to Scripture. Job 12:11 states, "Does not the ear test words as the tongue tests food?" (NIV). It is also wise to consult with other Christians if there is any question about the validity of what we have heard. "Where no counsel is, the people fall: but in the multitude of counsellors there is safety" (Prov. 11:14).

Vera, the woman described in chapter 6 who lost her son when she fled without him from an abusive husband, attended one of the CLASS sessions when Marilyn presented this prayer message. Afterward Vera wrote,

> I've realized over the years that I have a lot to share but have never been able to get it out. I've felt blocked . . . nothing seemed to flow. I chalked it up to "God's timing." During the guided prayer time

led by Marilyn Heavilin last Wednesday afternoon, during the time of "correction" when Marilyn asked us to ask the Lord to show us His view of us and give us a correct view of ourselves, I remembered the time twenty-five years ago when my ex-husband tried to strangle me. He stopped just short of killing me. In the prayer time, the Lord was with me and in my mind I could see Him take my ex-husband's fingers from around my neck! It wasn't until this morning that I realized why, at long last, I've finally been able to sit down, pull together thoughts on what to speak about, and begin writing brief summaries and an information sheet. I attribute this directly to the healing of that memory during the CLASS prayer time.

Please ask the staff to pray for me that the Lord will use all that's now released after being "strangled off" for so long and that God's creativity will flow through me to be a source of healing in the lives of others. Praise to His name! Now I can dare to dream of being a speaker for Him.

Vera now has a deep, two-way prayer life. As God gave her a quick answer to her concerns, he also healed her memory and set her free.

Seeing the World through God's Eyes

Dear Florence:

This is a praise letter mostly, not a question. God has already answered many of my questions. During the CLASS prayer lesson, I realized I had not been praying for my son. I was having trouble relating to my teenage son and during the section on correction I asked the Lord to let me see my son as he sees him, not from my own point of view. Immediately I saw my son as a lonely boy without real friends. He was standing on a beach, looking out to sea, and I began to cry for him. I'd never seen him that way before and I began to pray in earnest that I could reach out to him, that I could have a new understanding instead of a critical spirit, and that he would get a real friend. I can hardly believe how quickly the Lord answered me when I asked to be able to relate to my son. I have a much better relationship with him now that I am in tune to his needs, and as a bonus God gave my son a special friend. I no longer talk about prayer, I pray.

Becky from Boston **189**

What a testimony to the power of prayer and seeing the world (and those you love) through God's perspective!

Tapping into the Power of Prayer

One evening after a CLASS seminar Monica shared with our staff how much she had enjoyed CLASS and how restful it had been for her. Since CLASS is very intense training, conferees seldom use the word *restful* in describing the seminar. So we all laughed, and I commented, "Your life must really be hectic for CLASS to seem restful."

Monica smiled and said, "Hectic is an understatement. My husband has just sued me for divorce and he is doing everything he can to make my life a hell on earth."

Monica's husband of more than twenty years had apparently been planning the divorce for quite some time. He had managed to shift all their finances to his control, and he had even turned in a change of address for Monica at the post office so he would receive all of her mail, apparently to make sure she had no financial holdings he hadn't claimed yet.

Monica told how he was spreading lies about her to ruin her reputation and make things look better for him in court. Marilyn suggested that as Monica prepared for court she should pray that only the truth would be spoken. If her husband began to speak anything but the truth, she should pray that God would confuse his words so they would be completely ineffective.

Dear Florence:

Remember when I came to CLASS and told you it was restful? You laughed because no one but me thought the three days of training was restful. I was going through a divorce at the time, and sitting there in a protected environment was the most peace I'd had in months. It was suggested to me that at the trial I pray for my husband to be confused if he told anything but the truth. You won't believe this (actually, you will) but that's just what happened. He stood up and each time he began to lie, he stumbled and stammered, unable to get the words out. When he tried to accuse me, his words were jumbled and finally, in frustration, he stopped talking and sat down defeated. I've learned that there is power in prayer and that when God is on your side there's no such thing as helplessness. That knowledge has changed my life!

Monica from Montrose

Praying with Fervor and Faith

I became acquainted with Linda and Ron at a business seminar a few years ago and was shocked when I heard this news about them some time later. In a head-on collision with a van, Linda was thrown out the door of her car. She remembers the feeling of flying through the air and landing in a ditch. Her husband, Ron, who was asleep on the passenger side, was hurled through the windshield and landed face-down in a deep mud puddle. Their car was so totally destroyed that the police didn't think anyone could have escaped alive. They found Ron first and pulled his face out of the mud so he could breathe. Then the police searched around, eventually finding Linda, who was praying silently in the ditch, unable to make a sound. When I talked with Linda herself, she said, "The first thing I had to do was accept the reality that I was in a ditch and that I was alive. I couldn't see and I couldn't move, but I knew I was alive."

By the time Linda arrived at the hospital her eyes were swollen shut. One eye was pushed back into her head behind shattered facial bones. Upon examining Linda, the doctors found several breaks in her back and one leg so smashed that the bones were in splinters. Linda was put in a body cast and leg casts and awaited eye surgery. Her pain was beyond anything she could have imagined, and she could barely see through a slit in her good eye.

Through this experience Linda learned to pray with fervor and faith believing that the Lord was going to restore her health in His time. "He must have something great in mind for me or He wouldn't have kept me alive," she told me by phone. "It's a miracle that both Ron and I lived through what should have killed us."

When I asked Linda how she was getting through each day she explained that when she wakes each morning, she reestablishes the

191

reality of her situation. She doesn't deny her pain or cry over it; she accepts where she is and then prays to move on.

"What has helped me the most is setting a realistic goal for each day," Linda said. "One day it's to move my right big toe, the next day to flex my wrist. I write the goal in big print on a piece of paper and when my mind wanders because of the medication, I pick up the paper and reread my goal."

Each day Linda forced herself to get in the wheelchair and move to a new spot so she wouldn't get overwhelmed with the bleakness of one hospital room. "It's a lot easier to just lie there, but I would get depressed if I couldn't see some people. Some days I would sit near the front door and watch the people—people wearing real clothes."

Linda started writing her prayers and keeping a journal of her feelings as soon as she could use her wrist. She couldn't read what she was writing, but she knew in the future, after the two scheduled eye surgeries, she would be glad she forced herself to record these difficult days and write to the Lord. Today Linda is again physically whole after years of physical therapy and constant prayer.

What can those of us who are not in a body cast, who are not in physical pain, who are not facing surgery, learn from Linda?

1. *Assess the situation realistically.* We should not deny we have problems or weep and wail as if we were chosen by God to suffer like Job. We must put our pain in perspective and look at our situation as God sees it.

Earlier I described Becky, who was having trouble relating to her teenage son. Just as Becky prayed, "Show me my son from your point of view, Lord" we must all seek God's perspective of our circumstances.

2. *Set a reachable goal each day.* When we are discouraged or depressed, things tend to seem impossible. We look at the whole world and know we are unable to right the wrongs or fight the foes. It's all too much for us to face. But could we determine to achieve one small feat a day, wiggle a toe, flex a wrist, get dressed, clean a closet? Could we write it down on a piece of paper and look at it now and then? Can we keep a positive focus on at least one poten-

tial? If Linda could scrawl out a goal and peer at it through a slit, couldn't we make some strides ourselves?

3. *Pray when it's not an emergency.* Linda prayed in the ditch when she thought life was over, but she also prays each day in a heartfelt cry to the Lord who saved her. An emergency prayer now and then is acceptable to the Lord as long as he knows who we are. It's a little late to get acquainted. Linda is writing her prayers each day even though the process is painful. She knows she needs to stay in close touch with her Lord.

4. *Get a new look on life.* When we get depressed, sometimes over trivial problems, we find it easier to stay in bed and not get dressed, but this lack of drive makes us feel worse about ourselves. If Linda could sit alone in a wheelchair and move herself from one spot to another, can't we "lift up our eyes to the hills from whence cometh our help"? Can't we move on and encourage someone else, as Linda learned to do in a traumatic situation?

5. *Ask a question of the Lord and listen.* Linda listened to God and waited patiently for his answer. Her recovery was not instant—no miracle healings—but as Linda says now, "the miracle is that I'm still alive."

Experiencing Personal Healing

When I first met Katie she had come to CLASS to improve her writing and speaking skills. She already was a leader among the women in her denomination, but she knew there was something missing in her ministry. Katie was sincere in her search and open to my suggestions. First, we looked at her personality strengths and weaknesses and saw that her Choleric need to be in control and make decisions was too strong for those she was hoping to inspire. Katie agreed to pray that the Lord would soften her nature and make her less adamant in her statements. She also asked that he would show her any other areas in her life where adjustments were needed.

It is amazing that when we genuinely want to know, pray believing God can speak to us, and then listen for his answer, he will respond. Katie heard from the Lord that she needed to examine her childhood hurts and pray through them. She was to cease denying the presence of her pain and get real.

If the Lord said that to you, would you act upon it? Katie did. Over several years I've observed the changes in her. I've seen her personality soften, her determination mellow, her marriage improve, her search reach conclusions, and her training succeed. Because she was willing to ask the Lord about his will for her life and then listen to his answers, Katie is a new person today, and she enjoys a deeper relationship with her Lord.

Katie wrote me on New Year's Day:

Dear Florence:

I want to report to you how I am doing as I know you pray for me. This year holds within its days many goals—personal and professional. However, I have only one New Year's Resolution: completion of the cycle of training as a Christian leader and speaker, using the lessons you have taught me.

Because you taught me to use words more effectively, my writing has improved and my outlines for public presentations come quickly (and have a better chance of being remembered by my audiences). You have given me healing information to foster hope, and I have experienced much personal healing because I've been willing to see my past pain and drop the present pretense.

When I first met you, Florence, I had pain in my eyes and in my life. Now, due to much prayer, trust in the One who lets no memory emerge before its time, and my willingness to let the river of life flow at its own pace—without my trying to cross its current, swim upstream, or move too fast ahead of the flow—I can rest in the Lord. While I have no complete picture of what this training at CLASS means for the future, it is enough to have completed it. Thanks!

Your friend, Katie

Glance at Circumstances, Gaze at God

Tricia has two daughters who have been on drugs, and she has had to learn unconditional love in each situation. She has been involved in their lives through arrests, court cases, forced counseling, and twelve-step programs.

After one of her daughters was placed on house arrest for two weeks, God showed Tricia she needed to take a new approach in her own personal devotional time and in her prayers for her daughter. Although she had been a Christian for many years, she had never read all of the Bible, so Tricia decided to read through the Scriptures using a one-year Bible. Each day after she read the Scripture passages, she wrote in her journal, noting the truths from Scripture that pertained to her daughter; then she spent as much time as she could in prayer. She also began using the book *Praying God's Will for My Daughter* by Lee Roberts in which he provides hundreds of Scriptures that parents can pray over their family members.[3] Often Tricia would spend hours simply praying Scripture, inserting her daughter's name where appropriate.

We had Tricia speak at a Promise of Healing Workshop and tell about her daily prayer time. She explained how prayer helped her change her attitude from blame and anger to power and joy, even in less-than-ideal circumstances. Her situation is different from the physical trauma Linda suffered in the car crash, but her process is the same. Each day she faces the reality of her family problems. She doesn't lie about them or deny them. She is honest with God and others. She has set a daily goal of spending time with God in prayer whether or not there is a current emergency. Tricia is not wallowing in self-pity; instead she is teaching workshops to other mothers who are in similar circumstances. Instead of wasting time yelling at your children and telling them how bad they are, pray for them.

Within four months of her daughter's house arrest, Tricia's daughter had renounced her lifestyle of drug use and made her peace with God. At the time of this writing, the daughter has been completely drug free for five years, is attending church regularly, and has a good relationship with her family. As Tricia spent time in prayer she learned how to model Christ to her daughter, and she now understands that God's Word is truly the sword of the Spirit. In Tricia's words, "I have learned to glance at my circumstances and gaze at God."

We won't know until we get to heaven why we can do our best and still have our children go astray, but we can't waste our time on self-pity. We must take control of our lives and come to our

Lord and Savior daily. We must wake up to the power available to us when we take the time to ask.

Our Goal: To Become like Christ

Dear Florence:

I want so much to have a closer relationship with Jesus, but I don't seem to make much progress. I know I should read the Bible more, but it doesn't seem to relate to me in a personal way. Is it just that I don't spend enough time or have I never taken the Christian life that seriously?

Lifeless in Laguna

Dear Lifeless:

You are like many who write to me about getting their spiritual lives in order. The Bible doesn't make sense to those who don't search for truth. When we read a verse or chapter, we must ask ourselves, "What does that day? What does that mean in the context of Scripture? And how does that apply to me?"

In Philippians 3:10 Paul sums up the aim of the Christian life: "All I want is to know Christ and to experience the power of his resurrection, to share in his sufferings and become like him" (TEV).

You've seen what it says. In the context Paul is aiming for the ultimate goal of becoming like Christ, and this applies to you in that you can follow Paul's four steps: (1) get to know Christ, (2) feel his power, (3) share in the sufferings of others, and (4) become like him.

For those of us who are functioning as believing Christians and yet not experiencing the excitement of a daily walk with the Lord, perhaps it's time to take control and get serious about our commitment. Like Paul, we need to get to know Christ. Paul had a passion to spend time with Jesus each day. He didn't wait until he was drowning in a shipwreck or hanging by a thread in a basket to call out to the Lord. Paul faced reality every day and yet was able to focus on the Lord and get to know Him intimately. How do we get to know someone? We have to spend time with him or her. Now for the personal application of this verse.

Let's assume that you and I look out our window one morning and see a moving van unloading next door, we instantly get curious. We peer through the curtains and make judgments on our new neighbors based on their furniture, their looks, their children, and even their dog. We have assessed their status before we've even met them, but we don't really know them. How can we get to know them? We have to go next door and introduce ourselves. We have to spend time with them and get acquainted. How do we get to know Jesus? We must spend time with him in daily prayer and Bible study. How many of us come to him when it's not an emergency? Are there some of us who just peek at Jesus through the curtain now and then to make sure he's still there? Do we have no more than a windowsill relationship with our Lord?

Paul not only spent time with him, but he felt his power. You can't feel the power of someone you don't spend time with or you are estranged from. Yet all of us know someone who makes us feel good, who lifts us up when we're together. That's what Jesus wants to do with those of us who care to get acquainted. Are some of us hoping to pick up the power while sitting next door? While looking through the lace curtains?

Paul was willing to share in the sufferings of others because he knew his Jesus in a personal way, and his single aim was to become like him. Even though human nature sends so many of us scurrying in the opposite direction to look out a different window with a better view, we need to discipline ourselves to look straight up to Jesus.

So, dear Lifeless, it's time to get a life! Take control of your life and take the time to know Jesus.

In this chapter we've seen several women who learned to do that by developing two-way communication with the Lord. The results have brought new strength, new courage, and new joy to their lives.

- Vera is free to get to know Jesus in a closer way and free of the anger and fear that filled her marriage to an abusive husband. She's no longer looking at the Lord through the curtain but face-to-face.

- Becky knows the power of the Lord to reveal her teenage son's needs in a clear scene with no curtains to confuse her.
- Monica has learned that God can draw a dark curtain across the mind of a liar and can confound the words of the wicked, as he did when she prayed for truth in the courtroom.
- Linda says she'll never complain about minor problems ever again. As she lay in constant pain recovering from the devastating car crash, she spent time with Jesus and experienced his power. Now she's well and can share her experience to ease the sufferings of others. Only those of us who have come through traumatic situations seem to have a heart for those in pain.
- Katie has heeded the Lord's answers to her questions and by doing so has become a new person, an instrument of his love as she continues her work in his ministry.
- Tricia still prays in intercession for her daughter, asking God to give the girl the strength to keep away from her former drug-dominated life. As Tricia spends time face-to-face with Jesus each day she feels his power to lift her up, and she is willing to share what she's learned to help in the suffering of others.

Scripture tells us that when we desire to know Jesus, get so close that we feel his power, and are willing to share in sufferings instead of turning the other way, we will ultimately become like him.

We women need to face reality, take control of our lives, and call on the power available to us when we genuinely care to know Jesus. Let's take the time to part the curtains and see Jesus face-to-face. Let's not say, "I'll pray about it." Let's pray!

Appendix

◆◆◆◆◆◆◆◆

A Comparison of Three Views

	World View	Balanced Christian View	Legalistic View
Women	All women should be out in the workplace fulfilling their potential. They should dress for success and keep up with the latest trends.	Intelligent women need to evaluate their situation. Family comes first but single mothers or those in debt may need to work at least part time. They should dress suitably for the occasion.	All women should be at home with their children. They should dress modestly, wearing highnecked blouses, avoid makeup, and eliminate jewelry.
Men	Men are inferior and often abusive. Don't let them get the best of you. Fight your way to the top and show them who's boss.	Even well-meaning men don't get it at times. We need to make ourselves clear and help them understand us.	Men are superior and God speaks through men to their wives, who must be quiet and obedient.
Emotional Needs	Think of yourself first. It's a dog-eat-dog world. If you don't watch out for yourself, who will?	We all have emotional needs and we should prayerfully find the source of our pain so we can bring it to the Lord for healing.	If you were really a Christian, you wouldn't have any emotional needs. God would have filled them all.
Dysfunction	Wallow in your miseries. Repeat your problems to all. There can't be a God or this wouldn't have happened to you.	Not all families are perfect but we need to look at the situation honestly, take human steps to improve our situation, and know that God won't allow us to suffer more than we can bear.	Deny any problems. Pretend you are happy. Don't let anyone know if you are hurt. God is testing your patience and building your character.

	World View	Balanced Christian View	Legalistic View
Husband's Accountability	Men can't be trusted. Watch him like a hawk. Check up on his every move. If you suspect he's unfaithful, hire a detective. If you mutually agree to date others and stay married, this will broaden your relationship.	Believe your husband is an honest, faithful man, but don't be so naive that you can't recognize obvious signs of infidelity. Face the problem immediately and don't just look the other way and hope things will be better tomorrow.	Marriage is built on trust. You should never check up on your husband. If you are the wife you ought to believe he will not stray. If you're suspicious, confess it quickly to the Lord as a sin. If he has an affair, accept it as God's discipline for you and forgive him.
Money Matters	Don't let him get his hands on your money. You earned it and you deserve to spend it whatever way you want. Take charge of the money as quickly as possible.	Decide together who has the time and ability to handle the family finances. Keep in touch and make major decisions and purchases in unity. Know where all the important papers are.	Only men should handle money. They should make all the decisions because God has appointed them to be ruler of the family. Trust your husband to do the right thing.
Submission	Women are now liberated and must make up for the years they have been demeaned by men. We've come a long way, baby, but not far enough. Don't let any man tell you what to do.	Scripture tells us to be submissive one to another and to put the other person's needs before our own. It does not teach that we women are to be doormats and refuse to use our minds. Submission doesn't mean stupidity.	The wife's role is to be the helpmate no matter what. Submission is God's plan for the woman and she must display a subservient attitude at all times. The man is the lord of the house and the woman is to do his will.

	World View	Balanced Christian View	Legalistic View
Physical Abuse	If he lays a hand on you, call the cops. Report him to the authorities. If he does it again, throw him out and consider divorce. Tell all your friends what a rat he is. Find a feminist counselor who will defend you.	If you are being hit, pushed, slapped, or beaten, you are being abused. Report the abuse to your pastor or counselor and don't make excuses for your husband's behavior. If abuse continues there needs to be a separation until appropriate help can bring about change.	If you had been more submissive and done what he wanted, he wouldn't have hit you. Realize this is your cross to bear and you will get your rewards in heaven. Don't let anyone know what he's done because you probably provoked it.
Verbal Abuse	If your husband yells at you, yell back! Always be thinking of what ammunition you can use against him. Learn some strong words that will stop him in his tracks. Tell your girlfriends; they don't like him anyway.	If your husband insults you, points out your faults in public, or demeans you in front of your children, this is verbal abuse. This shows his insecurities and probably reflects what he received as a child. Refuse to accept this harsh treatment, pray for wisdom, and seek counsel.	If your husband insults you, realize you have not been submissive enough. It is our place to accept whatever our husbands say because God speaks through them and is trying to teach us something. We should not think too highly of ourselves. Learn to grin and bear it and God will bless you.

	World View	Balanced Christian View	Legalistic View
Taking Advantage	Don't put yourself out for others; they don't appreciate it anyway. Why should you let these people into your house when they've never had you to theirs? Don't give a nickel to your adult children; you supported them long enough. It's time they grow up.	Be hospitable, but not foolish. Be in control of the situation and don't become the maid to your guests. Make basic rules for dinner hour, chores, and baby-sitting. Don't let visiting children trash your home. Set departure dates for guests, especially your own adult children. Help them financially in emergencies.	You are called to selfless service and must have the attitude of a servant. You must open your home to strangers, the lame, and blind. You must be sacrificial and put other people's needs ahead of your own. You must always keep the door open for your adult children, no matter how old they are, and continue to bail them out when they need money.
Divorce	Divorce is a legal option for troubled marriages. You can always get a divorce if you're not happy. It's better for the children if you separate than stay and fight.	Divorce is a last resort and should not be jumped into quickly. Seek legal counsel before it's too late. Have copies of all deeds, wills, and trusts, and know where they are. Be sure you have a credit card in your own name.	Christians never get divorced under any conditions. There is no divorce in the eyes of God. Watch out for divorced women. They're after your husband. It's better to take abuse than to separate.

	World View	Balanced Christian View	Legalistic View
Dating Again after Divorce or Widowhood	The sooner you get into the social scene the faster you will recover. Realize in today's world sex outside marriage is acceptable. If you live together you will save money and test your compatibility.	Don't rush into dating again. Realize not every man in the church singles group is a balanced Christian. Don't date—or marry—someone because the pastor says it's God's will. God can find you and tell you personally. Don't get quickly involved with a man and his children. Don't leave a new boyfriend alone with your children.	Trust all men you meet in church. Consider them as Christian brothers. Assume the pastor has divine wisdom in choices for your happiness.
Prayer	It doesn't hurt to pray, but be sure you take control of the situation. Don't just trust luck or expect God to change your circumstances.	Approach solutions with both prayer and action. *"Faith without works is dead."* Believe God hears and answers prayer. The *"fervent effectual prayer . . . availeth much."* Write your prayers as David did the Psalms. *"Pray without ceasing."*	When you pray about it, you don't need to do anything about it. Leave the praying to the clergy who know how to do it right. Prayer is more effective in church or at healing meetings.

Notes

Chapter 1: Back When Father Knew Best and We Left It to Beaver

1. Walter Shapiro, "The Birth and—Maybe—Death of Yuppiedom," *Time* (April 8, 1993): 65.
2. Ibid.

Chapter 3: Who Are All Those Dysfunctional People?

1. Mary Kay Blakely, "Psyched Out," *Los Angeles Times Magazine* (October 3, 1993): 28.
2. Dr. Harriet Lerner, *Dance of Deception* (New York: Harper Collins, 1993).
3. Sir Walter Scott, "The Lay of the Last Minstrel," stanza 17.
4. *New York Times* Service reported in the *Los Angeles Times* (October 3, 1993).

Chapter 5: Managing the Money

1. Shelby White, *What Every Woman Should Know about Her Husband's Money* (New York: Turtle Boy/Random House, 1992).

Chapter 6: When Submission Allows Abuse

1. *Time* (June 29, 1992).
2. Sarah Yang, "14% of Women in Emergency Rooms Reported Being Abused," *Lost Angeles Times* (August 5, 1998): A3.
3. Gail J. Koff, *Love and the Law* (New York: Simon and Schuster, 1989).

Chapter 7: Sticks and Stones Can Break My Bones, and Words Can Also Hurt Me

1. Isaac Black, *Assault on God's Image* (Winnipeg: Windflower Communications, n.d.).

Chapter 8: Is Someone Taking Advantage of You?

1. *Mirabella* (October 1993): 183.

Chapter 9: Dealing with Divorce and Widowhood

1. *Woman's Day* (May 27, 1986): 36.

2. Rose Sweet, *How to Be First in a Second Marriage* (Joplin, Mo.: College Press Publishing, 1998).

3. Ruth Jean Loewinsohn, American Association of Retired Persons, *Survival Handbook for Widows (and for relatives and friends who want to understand)* (Glenview, Ill.: Scott, Foresman and Company, Lifelong Learning Division, 1984), 33.

Chapter 10: I'll Pray about It

1. Oswald Chambers, *Our Brilliant Heritage,* quoted in Harry Verploegh, ed., *The Best from All His Books,* vol. 1 (Nashville: Oliver Nelson, 1987), 253.

2. Marilyn Willett Heavilin, *I'm Listening, Lord* (Nashville: Thomas Nelson, 1993). Used by permission.

3. Lee Roberts, *Praying God's Will for My Daughter* (Nashville: Thomas Nelson, 1993). Versions of this book are also available for praying for wives, husbands, sons, and for yourself.

Known universally as one of the leading experts on personalities, **Florence Littauer** has written more than twenty-five books and is a popular speaker for both church and business conferences. Her best-selling book about personalities, Personality Plus, has sold more than 600,000 copies. Florence and her husband, Fred, have been married for more than forty-five years and frequently speak at retreats and leadership seminars.

For information about seminars and workshops conducted by Florence, please call 1-800-433-6633.